SURVIVAL: Enduring to the End

By Don V. Richey, Jr.

xulon PRESS

Survival
Enduring to the End
by Don V. Richey, Jr.

Printed in the United States of America

ISBN 978-1-60647-598-0

www.xulonpress.com

Dedicated to my dad, Dr. Don V. Richey, who faithfully preached the gospel of Christ for over 60 years and who has been my mentor and spiritual hero.

Contents

❦

Acknowledgements

❦

Arpie Vermillion, a retired teacher of the old school of English grammar, and a very dear friend as well as my daughter's mother-in-law, personifies the term editor. She lovingly poured over this material and showed a great deal of compassion and patience with this writer. Credit for this work being comprehendible most assuredly should be given to her.

Thanks Arpie.

My daughter Jeana Vermillion, daughter-in-law Kristi Richey, and my wife, Shirley, have all labored and prayed over this manuscript. They have been my encouragers and critics. Without them this work would still be in my computer.

Finally, I express my love and gratitude to the members of the Eagle Heights Church of Southeast Texas for their continued encouragement for me to publish my teachings.

Introduction

❦

The destruction of the Twin Towers in New York City on September 11, 2001 established a benchmark by which mankind will measure its future. Journalists and reporters already use the phrase "per-9/11" to indicate that society has emerged from the Cold War environment of nuclear annihilation and has entered into the new era of radical terrorism. Post-911 societies will not know the security of treaties or negotiation that was once enjoyed by the majority of Western civilizations. Post-modern societies now find themselves in a state of shock and despair as they seek pathways through the maze of fear and uncertainty.

In the aftermath of 911, people wandered around in a daze not knowing what had happened. They were unsure of what to do or where to go. Terror of such magnitude had never entered their thoughts. Even after the first failed bombing of the World Trade Center in 1993, people were still astonished and unprepared for 911.

Likewise, in New Orleans when the levees broke during hurricane Katrina and left thousands without a place to live, people did not know what to do. They were unprepared for such a disaster, and people began to panic. Fear and frustration took a firm grip upon the heart of those affected directly by the horror. Blame and accusations flowed as deep as the waters within the city. Why were the people not prepared? What caused the abandonment of caution and readiness? The warnings had been there, but no one took them seriously.

The Bible gives similar warning of impending disaster and calamity, but some Believers give little attention to its warnings. Jesus strongly emphasized to His followers the need to be ready for the approaching tribulation, especially as the warning signs of the end of time begin to appear. He taught that those who were prepared and endured would be saved. However, much like the residents of New York and New Orleans who did not give much thought to the warnings signs of destruction, post-modern Believers live their lives oblivious to the coming tribulation. Few, if any, seriously take the words of Jesus as pertaining to their generation.

The citizens of New York and New Orleans felt that they did not have to be concerned with the warning. How ridiculous it was to prepare for disaster when the government was there to provide assistance and to pick up the pieces after the wake of destruction! Strangely, the majority of post-modern Believers seem to have adopted a similar strategy in facing the warning signs of the tribulation. Although, they do not think the government will deliver them from the coming terror, they have convinced themselves that God is going to take them out of the trial and tribulations of the end time. Therefore, there is no need for them to make any physical preparation.

Taking physical steps to endure the time of sorrow that is approaching this earth does not express a lack of faith in God's providence or care. On the contrary, such action confirms faith. How often have you heard, "Faith without action is dead?" Making a disaster plan, acquiring adequate supplies and equipment, and taking safety training, underscores an abundance of faith in obeying the teachings of Jesus.

It is my desire in writing this book to encourage the Body of Christ to prepare for the troubling days ahead. Whether they be days of natural disaster, acts of terrorism, or financial short-falls in the economy, Believers need to be prepared to endure physically as well as spiritually. In my work with the American Red Cross and the Community Emergency Response Team, I have witnessed the difference between families who had made preparations and had developed a personal disaster plan and those who had not. Even those who only had a basic plan show greater resurgence than those who made no preparations at all. You might not agree with my theology but surely you will agree that every Believer needs a Disaster Plan.

As you read the following pages, keep in mind that we are living in a new age that is filled with many wonderful prophetic fulfillments which point to the imminent Return of Jesus. Will He find any faith when He returns to receive his Church? Will He find Believers prepared and abiding? Will your lamp be trimmed and burning? Make plans to endure.

Chapter 1

The Enlightened Intellect

❧

For as long as man has been on earth, he has pondered the ramifications of the termination of life on the planet he calls home. Each passing generation seems to ponder the question of whether or not it will be the last to live here on this "big blue ball." The present generation differs little from those that preceded it. Speculations concerning greenhouse gases, nuclear war, and overpopulation have added to the general fear among the populace about the inevitable destruction of planet earth. A quick glance at the tabloid headlines at any super market checkout reveals the concern that some have that aliens from space or some supernatural cosmic force will destroy life as we know it today. Movies flash across the silver screen portraying epic encounters with dooms-day as mortals defend the planet and save it from annihilation. From politics to pulpits, from coffeehouses to statehouses, and from living rooms to boardrooms, discussions about the end of time occur over and over again.

From the preeminence with which this subject dominates the mind of post-modern man, one might believe that concerns about global annihilation are a contemporary phenomenon, but their roots are deeply embedded in the history of human thought. Predictions and descriptions of global annihilation found in many, ancient writing, point to the overriding concern most, early civilizations held concerning the extermination of life on Earth. In spite of the intellectual or cultural differences of these diverse groups, they seemingly agreed that the world would one day come to an abrupt end. The Maya Indians of Central America were so influenced by the cataclysmic prophecies taught in their religion that they marked their calendar for the world to end in the year 2014.

Even the early Jewish Scriptures reveal a belief in the destruction of the earth, and forewarn those who place faith in God to be ready for such a day. Both Old and New Testament writers concur that the world will one day come to an abrupt end. Known as the "Day of the Lord" in the Old Testament and as the "Coming of the Lord" in the New Testament, the scriptures warn of the destruction and judgment that is associated with this catastrophic event. These writings provide ample instructions for Believers concerning what they need to do as they see these days of judgment approaching (Hebrews 10:25).

Understanding biblical messages concerning the End Time and the events leading up to judgment of God challenges even the most learned scholar. Many Christians avoid personal study of this topic simply because they are convinced that they do not possess the capacity to understand apocalyptical scriptures. They have made up their minds that the Bible contains so many ambiguous and secret-coded phrases that ordinary people cannot comprehend the mystery of its prophetic writings.

The Apostle Paul assured the common man that he could understand scripture not because he was intelligent but because he possessed the Holy Spirit. Paul once told his readers that being a part of the intellectual elite was not a pre-curser for being a Believer. He reminded the Corinthians that very few "wise men after the flesh are called but God hath chosen the foolish things of the world to confound the wise and God has chosen the weak things of the world to confound the things which are mighty (1 Corinthians 1:26-27)." However, in 1 Corinthians 4:10, Paul stated, "You are wise in Christ." Paul made his point very clear by often emphasizing in his letters that one did not have to be a scholar to understand the ways of God.

In Matthew 11:25, Jesus makes the same point when He says, "(God) has hid these things from the wise and prudent and hast revealed them unto babes." Comprehension of scripture lies not in one's intellectual expertise but in one's spiritual enlightenment, which comes through the illumination of the Holy Spirit. Jesus authenticated this in John 14: 26, when He said, "… the Comforter, which is the Holy

Spirit whom the Father will send in my name, He shall teach you all things."

The first people who read Revelation were not educated theologians but common, ordinary people who for the most part had little or no formal schooling. They quickly grasped John's message, which enabled them to withstand the Roman persecution and establish a flourishing Church in the midst of great suffering and trial. They lived every day to its fullest, while at the same time looking for the Lord's return and the end of the world.

The discernment of any biblical text demands divine enlightenment rather than great human intellect. God speaks to the heart of man through His Holy Spirit. The renewing or changing of the mind remains the responsibility of the individual Believer (Romans 12:2). To hear what the Spirit says, requires faith, not intellect. It requires a willingness to hear what the Spirit has to say even if the message is not popular or pleasing to the ears of men. Biblical interpretation should not be determined by the consensus of men but rather based upon the "thus says the Lord" confidence which the Holy Spirit gives.

Believers today, much like their counterparts of the first century, live life to its fullest, but in contrast, fail to give the return of Jesus much consideration. It is not that post-modern Believers reject the Second Coming of Jesus. That would be blasphemous. What they fail to do, however, is place confidence in the Holy Spirit to instruct them concerning this matter.

Any investigation into the arena of End Time events begins with asking questions. Jesus said, "Ask

and it shall be given unto you, seek and you will find."
When one studies the scriptures, the Holy Spirit
stirs the heart to question the status-quo of Biblical
interpretation. Like the Bereans of old, post-modern
Believers must search the scriptures to see if these
things which are being taught concerning the End of
the Age align with biblical text (Acts 17:10-11).

Eschatology, the intellectual study of the End
Time events in relation to biblical prophecy, seeks to
present and answer questions that arise from the study
of Scripture. It seems, however, that this intellectual
investigation creates more overwhelming questions
than valid answers. New theories concerning the
order of events which will mark the beginning of the
end often stir up confusion instead of sharing any
new light upon the perplexing apocalyptic events in
question.

The vast number of eschatological theories
from which a Believer can choose creates an overwhelming and very perplexing dilemma. The three
major theories accepted by most theologians include
the Amillennial, Postmillennial and Premillennial
views. There also exist the non-rapture, pre-rapture,
mid-rapture, and post rapture premises as well as the
half-rapture and full rapture theory.

Like a child in front of a candy counter, many
Believers become so intimidated by the vast number of
choices available that they grab something that looks
good without thinking. Others, afraid of accepting
the wrong theory, walk away empty handed.

Are all these theories wrong or do they, in some
way, contain some essence of truth? Can only one

theory be right? How can one know which theory is closest to what will really happen?

When looking at the smorgasbord of apocalyptic theories which are spread upon the eschatological table of post-modern thought, these and may other questions arise. They leave the Believer frustrated, at best. Why are there so few clear, concrete answers to these eschatological questions?

First, it must be remembered that Eschatology is a subjective science which is based upon suppositions rather than objective facts. Therefore, no theory can be 100% correct and none will be completely wrong. In some respects all theories hold some truth. Second, bear in mind that truth, for the most part, has been connected to popular consensus. Therefore, the post-modern church connects truth with popularity, and not necessarily with what is correct.

As a trend, Post-Modern Christians seemingly avoid digging into the truth concerning the End Time. Instead, they quickly embrace a theology which offers less suffering and sacrifice.

The pre-tribulation Rapture is a very popular theory among Believers today. It teaches that the Church will be snatched up out of this world just before the tribulation, thereby avoiding the troubles and sorrow that will be inflicted upon the earth during that time. This pre-tribulation Rapture theory offers a faith which is exempted from any trial or suffering. It offers a faith void of suffering and shame. Is there any wonder that this theory is so popular? But, if this is what really is going to happen, why does the Bible speak so much about the endurance of the

Saints? Why does it contain so many verses about being prepared and being "faithful until the end" if Believers are not to be left here on earth during the time of testing and purging? The answers to these questions strike a deafening silence. They are like the elephant in the room which no one talks about, failing to address the elephant will not make it go away or disappear. Ignoring the hard question resolves nothing. However, taking up such questions seemingly sends seismic tremors throughout the mountain of eschatological hypotheses.

The very thought of questioning such a popular theory seems ludicrous to some. To suggest that so many people have failed to interpret scriptures correctly seems to reflect an arrogant bias by those who would dare raise such a question.

"How dare you," some would say, "to question the popular preachers of today who teach pre-rapture theory as fact? How dare you to indicate that they are liars and deceivers?" Some preachers are so insecure in their belief of what they preach that they label any who question them as heretics. However, to raise questions of concern about the Word of God should not cause one to be labeled a false prophet or anti-Christian. Some have failed to ask question concerning apposing views in fear of being ridiculed or abandoned by their denominational leaders.

To ask questions concerning a certain biblical theory should not be considered a rebuke or rejection of orthodoxy, but rather, as an inquiry into the truth. Seeking the answers to difficult questions leads eventually to the truth, and as we know, the "Truth will set *us* free". Asking right questions leads to right answers.

A few questions which need to be considered are:

- "Why are there so many scriptures dealing with the End Time if Believers, to whom the Bible was written, escape all the pandemonium?"
- "If such scriptures were given as a warning to the unbelieving world, why then were they written to Believers?"
- "Why would a Believer be concerned about the tribulation or need to know anything about it if they are not to experience or need to prepare for it?"

To say that scriptures concerning the end of time were written to persuade the lost to avoid those dreadful days is to place little significance upon the prospects of Hell. The tribulation lasts only for a short period of time. Hell, the great deterrent, continues forever.

Assuredly, the main reason that such a large percentage of scriptures deal with End-Time events is simply because of grace. Throughout the pages of history the Lord has always been faithful in warning those who were about to experience His judgment. He desires none to perish.

The Lord faithfully gave each generation a warning before He passed judgment on them. The warning of approaching judgment to this present generation has been given in the form of fulfilled prophecies concerning world events and the glorious rebirth of Israel as a nation. Not only can the post-modern church observe the prophetic events happening before their very eyes, they can also compare the apocalyptic outline found in scripture with the last two thousand years of world history and see that with divine accuracy what God said would happen has come to pass!

These are the days of enlightenment. These are the days of revelation. At no other time in Church history has so much been revealed through the fulfillment of Biblical prophecy. The Church of this age, above all others, is without excuse for not being ready for the time of testing that is quickly approaching. The Bible tells us that to whom much is given much is required. Much will be required of the present day Church.

This generation has experienced so many fulfillments of End Time prophecies that it has almost become indifferent toward them. The fulfillment of prophetic scriptures has become so commonplace that Believers are no longer motivated by them to prepare themselves for what lies ahead. They have become prophetically numb to the events in the Middle East and to the posturing of nations lining up against Israel. They wait in a drowsy, spiritual slumber, anticipating the sound of the trumpet of God to awake them up just in time to be called home and out of all the mess.

The Day of the Lord will no doubt be a time of great sorrow and trials, but where does the Word of God say that the Church will not have to endure hardships or suffer during this period of time? The

Bible assures us that those who place their trust in the Blood of Jesus will be called up to meet the Lord in the air and there forever be with Him. The Word of God gives the Believer great assurance that he will not have to experience the wrath of God when, in the last days, He pours out His indignation upon all the earth (Romans 5:9).

Jesus bore the anger of God on the cross and all who place their trust in His sacrifice will escape the wrath that is to come. However, a careful study of scripture reveals that the tribulation period consists typically of the wrath of Satan and not the wrath of God. Before the wrath of God is released upon the earth, the Church will be raptured. This is the ultimate hope of all who believe in the Lord Jesus Christ. However, before the Rapture there first must be the purification of the Bride. Has the Church forgotten that the Second Coming of Jesus is about judgment?

One perplexing question which has been habitually avoided strikes at the very soul of the Church. Pulpits across the centuries have been quiet about how Believers should prepare for the Coming of Jesus. Peter was not apprehensive concerning the subject when he asked, "Seeing then that all these things shall be dissolved, what manner of persons ought ye to be in all holy conversation and godliness, looking and hastening unto the coming of the day of God wherein the heavens being on fire shall be dissolved and the elements shall melt with fervent heat (2 Peter 3:11, 12)."

What "manner of persons" should Christians be as they see the approaching judgment of the Lord?

Shouldn't they be, above all people, prepared? For the most part, however, they remain in a theological slumber, unaware and unprepared for the approaching trials. It is time to awaken from this slumber of false comfort and prepare for the approaching trials of faith.

In verse 14, Peter continues with his instructions to Believers concerning the Coming of the Lord: "...seeing that ye look for such things, be diligent that ye may be found of him in peace, without spot, and blameless." Using these three directives - being diligent, being at peace, and without blame - the following chapters endeavor to present the over-looked mandate to Believers concerning their preparation for the Coming of the Lord. Open your heart to the probing of the Holy Spirit. Search the scriptures to see if these things which will be discussed are true. But, above all, get ready for the coming of the Lord.

Chapter 2

Revival of Fear

❧

The rapture of the church, as described by Paul in 1 Thessalonians 4:17, remains an undeniable truth of scripture. The Bible, however, does more that provide substantial evidence of the "snatching" out from the world of the Blood-washed Saints of Faith. It gives insight as to when it will happen. No one knows the day or the hour of the Rapture, but Holy Scripture reveals numerous indications about the timing of this miraculous event and in graphic detail describes many of the corresponding events that will be associated with its occurrence.

Roman 5:9, tells us that through the Blood of Jesus we are saved from the Wrath of God which will be poured out upon all the earth in the last days (Revelation 16). This assurance of Paul indicates that the Rapture will occur before God sends His angels of wrath to defeat the Anti-Christ and his followers.

Therefore, Believers should not fear God's indignation, which will fall upon the enemies of Heaven, but
should hold a dreadful concern for the chastisement
that will fall upon the Church just before His wrath
is unleashed.

On the Mount of Olives, as recorded in Matthew
24, the disciples came to Jesus privately and asked
him when those things would happen about which
He had prophesied. They wanted to know what
would be the sign of His coming and the end of the
world. Although they asked three different questions
concerning what is now called the "end time", Jesus
answered all three inquires in one response. Studying
His answer reveals that there is an ascending order
of occurrence which shows an orderly progression of
events that must take place before the end can come.
Jesus divided His answer into three separate divisions
which He labeled "the beginning of sorrows" (birth
pains, verse 8), time of "great tribulation" (verse 21),
and "the sign of the Son of man" (verse 30).

Jesus taught that there would be a time of sorrow
which would cause great affliction upon the church.
The use of personal pronouns in verses four through
fifteen reveals the exclusive nature of the warning
that Jesus was giving to His disciples. This is the
beginning of "birth pains" that the Church will
experience before the Rapture. The next segment,
Jacob's troubles, confronts the Jewish community
and describes the slaughter that will come upon the
seed of Abraham. The last segment of the Lord's
revelation concerns the unbelieving world and the
disaster that will befall the "tribes of the earth" as

God Almighty brings an end to the rule of Satan over the kingdoms of the earth.

Some Bible students only see two divisions in this passage, thereby, failing to see the "Days of Sorrow" as a separated entity. The Lord makes it very clear by His choice of pronouns that the church will have to endure these days of sorrow and those who endure to the end will be saved. (We will discuss the meaning of "being saved" within this context a little later.)

Jesus warned the church about the persecution that would come against it at the end of the age. There is no question of the fact that in Matthew 10:21-22, Jesus was addressing Believers when He warned them of what would happen near the end of time by saying, "And brother shall deliver up the brother to death, and the father the child: and the children shall rise up against their parents and cause them to be put to death. And ye shall be hated of all men for my name's sake: but he that endures *(Gk. hoopmeno)* to the end shall be saved." Again in Matthew 24: 13, Jesus said, "But he that endure *(Gk. hoopomeno)* unto the end, the same shall be saved."

This same message of the Lord finds its way into the letters written to the seven churches of Asia Minor which John recorded in the book of Revelation. The only difference between the Matthew and Revelation texts are two different, yet similar, Greek words which translate into the English as "endure" and "overcome". In Revelation the Lord uses the term *nika*o, the Greek word for "overcome", rather than *hoopomeno* which is *the Greek* term for "endure".

The Lord says, in Revelation. 2:10 "...He that overcometh (nikao) shall not be hurt of the second death."

A word study of these two Greek terms, *hoopomeno* and *nikao,* offers an unmistakable awareness of the warnings that Jesus gives to the Church as it approaches the end of the age. *Hoopomeno* can be, and perhaps should be, translated "remain" rather than endure. The word can also be translated as "linger behind." Both interpretations reveal a Church that remains during the "beginning of sorrows." The word *nikao,* which comes from the Greek word *Nike,* relates to a victory or conquest. *Nikao* could be translated prevail, as in a struggle against an enemy, or to win the victory.

Applying these new translations to scripture helps clarify the warning that the Lord gives to the Church. It confirms with some reassurance that the Church will remain under the trials and testings during the pre-"great tribulation" period. Believers must endure this period of testing and purging as Christ purifies His Bride. It will be a time of struggle, but for those who are prepared for the attacks and deception of the Antichrist, it will be a time of victory.

These days of sorrow described by the Lord reveal a terrible sequence of events that will try the Church and purge it of the tares that have been mingled in with the wheat. Jesus described this first half of Daniel's last prophetic week as being filled with deceptions, wars and rumors of war, pestilence, and earthquakes. Yet, in introducing the great tribulation, Jesus gives His greatest description of what the "Days of Sorrow" will look like. Of the great tribulation Jesus said that "not since the beginning of the world has there been such tribulation, therefore leaving open the "Days of Sorrow" for anything that has already happened on earth. What could these days of sorrow hold for the Church? What could happen in the preceding days before conditions really get bad? To these questions Jesus leaves the door wide open to anything that has occurred before in the history of mankind.

The Flood will not be repeated, for the Lord promised Noah that He would not destroy the world by water again, but this does not exclude floods of local devastation. One will notice that many of the plagues of Revelation replicate those that came against Egypt in the days of Moses. Remember that the Israelites lived through these plagues.

The cruel attacks by the Assyrian and Roman armies upon the Jews still cause civilized man to wonder at the vulgar brutality that they demonstrated. However, in today's sophisticated world, the Church has already felt the brutality of homicidal terrorist who would as readily cut off the head of a woman or helpless baby as they would kill a stray dog. Much of what the Church in third world is experiencing in the twenty-first century resembles the brutality perpetrated against Jerusalem by the ancient armies of Assyria and Babylon.

Could a resurgence of the Crusades be part of these days Christ called "the Days of Sorrow"? What about wars? We have had two great world wars in the twenty century. The last one ended with a nuclear exchange that killed thousands.

As the twenty-first century advances, rogue nations like North Korea reveal that they have the ability to use nuclear weaponry. Iran seeks frantically to obtain such knowledge and ability. Will there be a nuclear war in the near future? Could there be another holocaust awaiting the seed of Abraham?

All this could happen at the beginning of the end, within the time period described by Jesus as the "Days of Sorrow." Verses four through fifteen of the Olivetti Discourse speak directly about pre-rapture events which the Church will experience. The tragedy is not so much that the Church will be purged as that Christians are unaware of the trials they must face.

Jesus encourages the Church that goes through the period of sorrow by saying that He would come quickly and take them out of the world (Matthew 24:22). He has promised that He will not put more on His children than they can bear (1 Corinthians 10:13). In Revelation 2:10, The Lord tells the church at Smyrna that they will be in tribulation for ten days. This measured time span reassures the Church that it can endure the trials of testing that will come upon it.

But, how long is this ten day period in apocalyptic time? When will these ten days start? Does the Bible give us any answers to these questions? Yes, it does!

The tribulation period, which includes the time the Lord calls "the Beginning of Sorrows" and the "Great Tribulation", covers a period of seven years, as prophesied by Daniel through his vision concerning the 70 weeks (Daniel 9:24). All of the weeks of which

Daniel prophesied have been fulfilled except for one. That week, which is called "the Tribulation", will be divided into two divisions of 3½ years each. The first 3½ years will be known as a time of wars and rumors of war, famines, pestilence and earthquakes. Jesus said that this will be a time when the world will seek peace but will find it unattainable. In the last 3½ years of Daniel's final week, Satan focuses his diabolical envy against all Jews and Christians as he establishes himself as a god, demanding the whole world to worship him and take his mark. Somewhere in the midst of this Great Tribulation, the Church will be raptured. Therefore, the ten days spoken of in Revelation 2:10 will be a period of time that follows the revealing of the Antichrist.

By studying the history of Israel in relationship to the time periods represented by Daniel's prophecies, scholars discovered that a prophetic week consists of a cluster of seven years. Understanding this helps to comprehend the message Jesus gave to the church at Smyrna when He said, "…and ye shall have tribulation ten days… (Rev.2:10)."

Do these ten days equate with Daniel's prophecy in that they represent ten years? There are those who interpret it this way and believe these were the ten years of persecution the Church suffered at the hand of Rome. However, such a view lacks substance in that the first century church suffered more than ten years of persecution at the hands of the Romans.

Jesus told John in Revelation to write about three different time periods. He was to write about things which have been seen, things which are, and things which are to come (Rev. 1:19). The "ten days of tribulation" fall under the last part of this outline: "things which are to come." At the time of the writing of Revelation, the Church was already under harsh persecution. The warning about "ten days of tribulation" would not apply to that time period. The destruction of Jerusalem in 70 A.D. began the march of cruelty against Jews and Christians by Rome. John's imprisonment on Patmos was a result of this brutal persecution. John wrote the Revelation in 95 A.D., some sixty plus years after the death of Christ.

These "ten days of tribulation" which Jesus refers to assuredly relate to the tribulation of the end time period which apply to "that which shall be hereafter." But, how do they apply into the framework of Daniel's prophecy regarding the 70 weeks?

It might appear impossible to determine how these ten days may actually relate to a prophetic time table but by using Daniel's analogy of a week being seven years, a proportional equation can be developed between days and weeks. Such a proportion would assume a day as being twenty-four weeks. In other words, ten days would amount to a total of two hundred and forty weeks in apocalyptical writings. Dividing fifty-two (the number of weeks in a year) into two hundred and forty, a time span of about four and two-thirds years emerges. If this is the case, the Lord is warning the Church that it will go through four and a half years of Tribulation which will include a year into the Great Tribulation. Therefore, the Church would know the Antichrist and would have to choose between taking his mark and worshipping his image or risk being put to death. Reading the last portion of the tenth verse reveals that this is exactly what the Lord had in mind when he said, "be thou faithful unto death and I will give thee a crown of life (Revelation 2:10)."

Jesus said that "for the elect's sake those days shall be shortened." Because of the marvelous Grace of God, these days of trial and purging will be shortened. Believers will not have to suffer like the lost but they will know a time of testing that will prepare the Bride for eternity. The Church will not experience the wrath of God for, by His grace, He will take it out of the world before His indignation will fall upon the unrighteous. The Church will be saved even as by fire (1 Peter 1: 7; 1 Corinthians 3:15).

Remember Jesus also said that, "as the days of Noah were, so shall also the coming of the Son of man be. For as in the days that were before the flood they were eating and drinking, marrying and giving in marriage until the day that Noah entered the ark and knew not until the flood came and took them all away so shall also the coming of the Son of man be (Matthew 24: 37-39)."

Jesus makes it very clear that the very day that Noah was placed into the ark, the wrath of God fell (also see Genesis 8:11-13). Likewise, the very moment that the Church is taken out of the world through the Rapture, the wrath of God will fall. Jesus said that the wicked world knew not that Noah had been shut into the ark (vs. 39) until the judgment fell. There will be no time for the non-believers to recognize that the Church had been raptured for, simultaneously, God's wrath will fall.

The final week (seven years) of Daniel's prophecy focuses upon judgment. It is all about judgment: judgment of the nations, of those who rejected Christ, judgment of Believers and the Angels. All will be judged. Paul emphasizes that all, believers and non-believers, will be judged by Christ (Matthew 25:32; Acts 10:42; Romans 14:10; 2 Corinthians 5:10). Paul underscores this argument when he writes in 2 Corinthians 5:10, "Knowing therefore the terror of the Lord we persuade men...." Again in Hebrews 10:31 we read, "It is a fearful thing to fall into the hands of the living God". But where has the fear of God gone? Has it already been raptured? Who fears His judgments anymore? Surely, not the pre-tribulation rapture theorist. Their teachings seem to indicate that the Church needs not fear any chastening of God for it will skip that dreadful time of sorrow and purging.

The Bible clearly teaches that the fear of God is the beginning of wisdom but when the post-modern Church begins to seek wisdom concerning the End Time, fear is the first thing they discard. No wonder there is so much confusion concerning the topic.

The study of eschatology must be done in "fear" of the Lord. To eliminate the fearsome judgments of God in association with End Time prophecies will lead one into an erroneous conclusion. But, has the fear of the Lord already been taken out of the Church? Has there already been a "great falling away" from the fear of the Lord among Believers?

Listen to the thunder of the approaching rain. Hear the rumble of judgment. Allow the Word of Truth to shake you with fear at the righteous judgments of a Holy God. Then you will comprehend, with wisdom, the scriptures concerning the "Last Day."

Chapter 3

Lessons in Preparedness

❦

After the destruction of the twin towers on 9/11, America, and for the most part, the rest of the world, lives with a nerve-wrenching anticipation waiting for the next shoe to fall. The evil minds of terrorists plot their diabolical plans for the annihilation of western civilization, overshadowing the peace and tranquility that once was enjoyed by most Americans. Dirty bombs with their nuclear fallout, biological contamination of drinking water and the food supply, and the threat of another terrorist attack against the infrastructure of the nation keep the average citizen on a relentless vigil.

Like the red horse of Revelation, the radical Muslim extremists have stripped the world of peace. In this war against terrorism, the front lines of combat find their way into every home and into every life. The next flash point could well be at work tomorrow, at the next football game, or Sunday morning at a church near you. But Jesus said "…see that ye be not troubled: for all these things must come to pass… (Matthew 24:6b)."

How can anyone not comprehend the fact that the "Time of Sorrow" which Jesus foretold, is approaching this present generation with unprecedented speed? The events in the Middle East demand our attention, as radical, Muslim nations line up militarily against Israel and prepare for a final showdown with Western civilization. We have little time to prepare and there is much to do. To set idly by and do nothing would be foolish and unwise.

In Matthew chapter twenty-four, Jesus revealed the chronological order of events which would lead up to His return to earth. Jesus calls the first wave of events "the beginning of sorrow" (vs.8). These days come just prior to the "Great Tribulation." The rapture of the Church, which marks the calling out of true Believers from this world, occurs somewhere following the "days of sorrow" and before the "wrath of God." The three parables found in Matthew chapter twenty-four, which follow the presentation of the chronological events of the end of the world by Jesus, should not be interpreted to suggest that salvation could be earned or achieved through some physical exercise of personal preparation. Salvation of the soul remains the work of grace. Ephesians 2:8 reads, "For by grace are ye saved through faith; and that not of yourselves: it is the gift of God: not of works, lest any man should boast." Therefore, these illustrations do not give instruction concerning the salvation of the soul but rather the need for a physical, bodily salvation. In Matthew 10:22 Jesus said, "He that endureth to the end shall be saved." Enduring saves the body, not the soul. To endure, however, one must be prepared for endurance. These three parables found in Matthew 24, focus upon preparedness. Everyone needs to be prepared for the "days of sorrow." This includes the lost as well as the saved.

In Philippians 2:12 Paul wrote, "Work out your own salvation with fear and trembling." Paul is not contradicting what he had earlier written to the Ephesians. Here he refers to a physical salvation of the body (health and welfare), and in Ephesians he refers to soul salvation (eternity). Being saved by grace does not release a Believer from the responsibility of being physically prepared for the coming of the Lord.

Notice the vocabulary which the Lord uses in these three parables (ex. virgins, servants and nation). This gives a clear understanding that preparedness, or lack thereof, does not alter the personal identity but does reflect the individual's integrity. In other words, they were foolish (lack of integrity) but they were still virgins (personal identity). They were evil and unprofitable, yet they were still servants.

The question is not whether one can lose his salvation because of ill preparedness but, rather, what quality of eternal life he will experience. Luke 12:47, records the warning of Jesus to those who are not prepared for His coming. He says, "And that servant, which knew his Lord's will and **prepared not himself**, neither did according to his will, shall

be beaten with many stripes (emphasis added)."
Unfortunately, most Believers have a very narrow
concept of eternity which does not, for some strange
reason, accommodate any punishment for the unprepared Saint.

The fact remains very evident that there are
foolish and unprofitable Believers who will suffer
because they are not prepared for the "Days of
Sorrow" or for "the Day of the Lord." Such foolishness does not eliminate their eternal status as children of God. Works or the lack thereof, does not
determine one's eternal salvation from Hell. That is
settled by the Blood of Jesus. Works only classify
whether a Believer is wise or foolish.

Many Bible scholars teach that the Rapture of
the church will come before the tribulation and that
Believers do not have to worry about the days of
trial and suffering. Therefore, they need not worry
or concern themselves about making any preparations to endure. They dismiss the warning of Jesus
as only applicable to Israel. Nevertheless, a faithful
and wise servant will be found ready and prepared at
all times.

Jesus unquestionably described the days which
the Church must be prepared to endure. According
to His teachings on the Mount of Olives, these days
will first be filled with wars and rumors of war. The
twentieth century experienced two great World Wars,
two Asian wars, and a Cold War. As the twenty-first
century begins, a third world wide conflict seems to be
on the horizon. Was this what Jesus was describing?

Next, Jesus said that "kingdom will rise against kingdom." Surely the Lord was not repeating himself. Kingdom against kingdom cannot be the same as "wars and rumors of wars." Redundancy of the matter would serve no reasonable conclusion, so this phase must have another meaning.

When Pilate asked Jesus if He was a king, the Lord replied, "My kingdom is not of this world." Paul identified the kingdoms that are against each other in Ephesians 6:12. "For we wrestle not against flesh and blood, but against principalities, against powers, against the rulers of the darkness of this world, against the spiritual wickedness in high places." The kingdoms that are against each other are the kingdom of light and the kingdom of darkness. Jesus refers to spiritual kingdoms. As the days of His coming draw near, great spiritual battles will be fought in the heavens and on earth. Some will be visible and some invisible (Colossians 1:16).

One would think, in this post-modern world of enlightenment, that spiritual persecution would be nonexistent; however, the contrary is true. Today, we see more religious persecution than at any other time in history. The Muslim kingdom is rising against the Jewish kingdom as well as against the kingdom of Christ. Thousands are killed throughout the world simply because they do not hold to an acceptable religious belief. Called genocide by the post-modern elite, this slaughter is no more than religious intolerance. Even western Christianity finds itself being attacked in what was once the home of free religious expression. As Jesus promised, kingdoms have already risen against kingdom.

The Lord continues His description of days of sorrow as being a time of famines, pestilences, and earthquakes. In other words, we will see great, terrifying environmental disasters in three areas: in the lack of food; in the plague of diseases; and in seismic activity and natural disasters.

The world is already preparing for the effects of global warming and the destruction of ozone layer. The Bird Flu and the devastation of AIDS are poised to develop into the worst pandemic the world has ever seen, which will be a terrible time for everyone. With the occurrence of earthquakes in strange places, such as the Oregon Coast, Illinois, and the Gulf of Mexico, this generation could well be witnessing the beginning of sorrows.

Is the Church ready for its time of testing and trials? Jesus makes it very clear that a faithful and wise servant will be ready, prepared, and waiting for the return of his Master. It is an unfaithful Church that sleeps, waiting to be awakened just in time to be snatched out of this world. The Church must remember that Jesus prayed that God would not take the Church out of the world but that it would be protected from evil.

"I PRAY NOT THAT THOU SHOULDEST TAKE THEM OUT OF THE WORLD BUT THAT THOU SHOULDEST KEEP THEM FROM EVIL, John 17:15."

The Church has been warned to be ready. It must be prepared, for no one knows the hour of the Lord's return. Faithfulness in preparedness remains a mandate from the Lord to His Church. Since preparedness reflects faithfulness, it is no wonder the Lord asked if He will find faith when He returns.

After answering the questions of the disciples concerning the end time, Jesus drives home the important issue for the disciples and the Church of today. In Matthew 24: 45, Jesus asked his disciples the rhetorical question, *"Who then is a faithful and wise servant?"* He quickly answers it in the next verse by saying, *"...he who is found doing what he has been instructed to do when his master returns (personal translation)."* Jesus then gave three parables to illustrate his point.

Since all three parables deal with reinforcing the same lesson, we must find the common thread that runs through each story if we are to understand His teaching. Unquestionably, that thread is preparedness: being ready for the coming of the Master. These lessons do not teach about placing faith in the Blood of Jesus for the cleansing from sin, which is essential for soul salvation. They teach rather about a physical salvation during the time Jesus calls the "Days of Sorrow." The preparation Jesus is teaching about is physical salvation, not spiritual restoration.

In careful study of these three parables, a vivid outline emerges that gives clear directives of how the Lord desires the Church to prepare for His Second Coming. These illustrations present a timeless three-point outline for preparedness. Each point of the outline reflects the main teaching from each of three parables. Altogether, they provide a simple but profound three-point strategy.

The first parable tells a story about ten virgins who went out to meet the bridegroom. When they were awakened at midnight to the sounds of the bridegroom's coming, they all began to trim their lamps. Five were called wise because they had oil in reserve and were able to light their lamps. Five were foolish because their oil had run out (Matthew25:1-13).

The second parable presents three servants who were all given talents according to their abilities. Two received praise from their master for increasing what they had been given while the third servant, known as the unprofitable servant, lost what he had and was cast into outer darkness simply because he did nothing with what he had been given. This parable develops the idea that one prepares for the return of the Lord by developing or increasing what he has been given (Matthew. 25:14-30).

The third and last parable focuses upon the nations of the world and how they treated those Jesus calls His brethren. We will see later that this is not a parable at all but a prophecy Jesus makes concerning those who do not care for the needs of Israel or Christians during the "Days of Sorrow" (Matthew. 25:31-46).

These three parables become a biblical guide for developing a three point outline for preparedness. Together, these three illustrative lessons present a clear mandate for the essential areas of preparedness; physical, spiritual, and social.

The parable about the ten virgins teaches the need for making physical preparation for the "Days of Sorrow." This parable teaches that a surplus of oil (or living supplies) needs to be accumulated before the coming of the Bridegroom. The oil in the parable represents physical provisions that maintain the quality and dignity of life. During the "Days of Sorrow," finding these things will be like the five foolish virgins searching at midnight for an oil merchant. Even if they are found, the price of any essential commodity at this time will be very costly.

The parable about the three servants who received the talents actually refers back to the introduction of a faithful servant found in Matthew 24:45. In this parable Jesus teaches about preparing spiritually for the millennium reign of Christ. This parable teaches that Believers are called to do more than a minimum service. In Matthew 5:41, Jesus teaches that His followers should go beyond that which is required by the Law. Christians have been called to go the second mile with others and with God. Simply doing what is required leaves no room for any admiration. In Luke 17: 9-10, Jesus makes this very clear when he says, "And the servant is not even thanked because he is merely doing what he is supposed to do. In the same way you obey me you should say, "We are not worthy of praise. 'We are servants who have simply done our duty' (NLT)". The King James Version puts it this way, "We are unprofitable servants: we have done that which was our duty to do."

The last parable in this trilogy is, actually, not a parable at all but rather a prophecy concerning the beginning of the millennium reign. Notice the word choice of Jesus in his introduction to each story. In the first parable about the virgins he begins by saying, "The kingdom of heaven is likened unto..." Here Jesus uses a simile in making a comparison. The next parable begins, "The kingdom of heaven is as..." Here Jesus uses a metaphoric statement to describe the Kingdom of Heaven and to give insight into the millennium administration and the consequences for those who live an unfaithful (unprofitable) Christian life. However, when he introduces the last parable, which is about the nations, Jesus says, "When the son of man shall come in his glory...." This is not a parable. This is a prophecy! No correlation, comparison, or analogies found here- just **FACT!**

One of these glorious days the sky is going to split apart like a parchment and the King of Kings and Lord of Lords will step from eternity into the present and once again place his foot upon this earth. This time, however, Jesus will be a conquering King, and will sit upon the throne of David, where He will rule for a thousand years.

This world is approaching the seventh millennium since the creation of man. Is this millennium the Lord's rest? Scripture teaches that a thousand years is but a day to the Lord (2 Peter 3:8). Scripture also teaches that on the seventh day the Lord rested. Is this generation on the edge of eternity? Will it see the coming of the Lord? Undoubtedly, it will, most definitely, experience the "Days of Sorrow." Jesus said in Matthew 24:34, "Verily, I say unto you that this generation shall not pass, till all these things be fulfilled." Get Ready!

Chapter 4

Don't Hurt the Oil

For as long as I can remember, the parable concerning ten virgins, which is found in the twenty-fifth chapter of Matthew, has captivated my imagination. For more than thirty years I have dedicated a considerable amount of energy studying the depths of this teaching of Jesus. In my bottom, right-hand desk drawer rests a worn out file folder with darkened, tattered edges. An adhesive label which bears the marks of a manual typewriter shows the stain of much handling and many years' study. Looking closely, one can make out two words: "Ten Virgins." Stuffed between the limp sides of this old folder lies a collection of articles, personal notes, and sermons which I have collected over the years in my study of these remarkable women who went out in the night to wait for a bridegroom to come home.

However, I always have felt that this parable contains much more than I have traditionally been told.

In my study of the parable about the ten virgins, I discovered that others also were seeking more from this lesson. I was exposed to an assortment of thoughts and conclusions. Some were worth noting while others left me wondering if the author of the article and I were reading the same passage. What became very evident in this search, however, was that there stirred a hunger among many in the academia of Christianity for more insight from this remarkable parable than that which was being routinely taught.

In my research I found that some held the opinion that Jesus was teaching about the infilling of the Holy Spirit. Because Jesus chose oil as one of the objects in the parable, they speculated that this must be a lesson about being filled with the Spirit of God before the Second Coming of Jesus. Although I find nothing analytically wrong with the thought of being filled with the oil of God (i.e. the Holy Spirit), such an interpretation fails the test of simple hermeneutics, the formal study of scripture.

First, it is obvious according to Acts 8:20, that the Holy Spirit cannot be bought nor sold. The virgins who ran out of oil were told to go and buy oil from those who sold it. The Holy Spirit is not for sale. Secondly, the Holy Spirit is the third part of the Triune God. Almighty God is not a commodity which can be bought or sold like a pound of sugar. Neither can He be stored up in some fruit jar for some future use. He is God, the Great I Am, flowing through the lives of His children like rivers of refreshing, living waters (John 7:38).

Another popular conclusion concerning this parable is that it contains truths concerning lost religious practitioners. This premise ventures to suggest that not every one who thinks they are saved are truly Born Again. To this I readily agree, but even though the theory finds support in other scriptures, this parable provides for it no scriptural foundation. The closest connection rests solely in the similarity of the reply given by the bridegroom to the five foolish virgins and that of Jesus in Matthew 7:23, when He said, "Depart from me for I never knew you: ...." Because of this one familiar link, some insist that the five foolish virgins must represent those who practice religion but are lost.

Without question there are those who claim the Name of Jesus who are no more born again than a broom stick, yet that has little to do with this parable. You see, whether foolish or wise, they were all still virgins. Being foolish did not alter their virginity. It did, however, cost them the privileges as virgins to welcome home the bridegroom.

As I studied the traditional explanation of the parable and how Jesus used it to illustrate the necessity of always being ready for His return, I came to understand that the focal point of the lesson really wasn't the virgins but rather the oil. The privilege of joining the bridegroom and his wedding party required that they indeed be virgins, but also, that they could provide lamps to light the way for him. Even though five of the ten girls were true virgins, they could not provide light for the bridegroom because of their lack of physical preparedness.

When I realized the importance of the oil in this parable, I began to understand that this was indeed an instruction about preparations; physical preparations. Being a virgin represented the spiritual preparedness but that fact never came into the discussion. The problem was not with their spiritual preparedness but with their physical readiness: they never stopped being virgins but they did run out of oil.

The human experience expresses itself in three areas of awareness: Body, Mind and Soul. Whereas Christianity embraces all three areas in its doctrine, duty and devotion, the majority of people consider that Christianity's only responsibility lies within the spiritual nature of life and therefore has no place in the physical or mental areas of the human experience. Be that as it may, Jesus had no problem merging the spiritual and physical within His teachings. Even though this parable touches on the spiritual responsibilities, its main focus zeros in on physical preparedness. The central theme of the parable does not center on the spiritual preparation of the girls (their virginity) but rather their physical preparedness or the lack thereof (no oil).

The oil within this parable signified a product of monetary value and physical survival. Considered as a commodity in Biblical days because of its ability to be bought, sold, stored or used, oil maintained itself as an essential element for survival. Any quality of life in ancient times required the possession of oil. The five foolish virgins had a limited amount of this precious commodity, which resulted in their predicament at midnight. They undoubtedly started out with much excitement and with lamps full of oil. In their excitement they failed to make plans for what they would do if they ran out of oil before the bridegroom arrived. As a result, they bore the condescending label of being foolish.

On the other hand the five virgins who received recognition as being wise refused to allow their excitement to deter them from making physical preparation in case the bridegroom tarried. In other words, they did not allow their emotional excitement to ignore the physical obligation, but appropriately, weighed them out. Because they possessed a reserve of oil, the five wise virgins were able to go out and meet the bridegroom while others had to "stop and go shop" at midnight.

As a sidebar to this, just let me add that oil you buy at five in the afternoon will always be cheaper than oil bought at midnight. Not only is it wise to have a reserve of commodities on hand for the unexpected events of life, it is also prudent.

As a commodity, oil represents the bare basis of human survival. During the Biblical period, the quality of life could not have been preserved with much dignity without this important staple. The fundamental nature of this fact surfaces within the ministry of the Old Testament prophet, Elijah. Two major events occurred within his ministry that emphasize the importance of oil in the daily life of biblical personalities.

One event tells of a widow who was down to her last handful of meal and last drop of oil. When she met Elijah she was gathering sticks to build a fire to cook her last meal. When asked to prepare food for the prophet, the widow had to use her last bit of oil and meal which meant that she and her son would do without. However, by obeying, she was rewarded by being able to return daily to the barrel of meal and to the cruse of oil and find provisions for nourishment. The oil produced by faith carried her and her son through the hard time of famine.

Later, Elijah met another widow who had just a little oil but a great, big debt. Her whole existence focused upon the amount of oil she possessed. Elijah told her to pour the oil she had left into as many empty vessels as she could find. After she had obeyed the prophet, she returned and told him that her little bit of oil had filled many empty vessels. Her worth and value had increased proportionally with the amount of oil she then possessed. Elijah told her to sell the oil and pay off her debt.

Within scripture are many insightful lessons on the significance of oil. It was used as fuel in lamps for light. It found uses for healing, in makeup, and food preparation. So important was oil in the survival of the human race that the angel in Revelations 6:6 told the fourth horseman, "Do not hurt the oil."

All this emphasis on oil does not teach that those who draw near to the "Beginning of Sorrow" should go out and store up barrels of olive oil. However, there here lies a fundamental lesson concerning storing up of those things that give quality and dignity to life.

During pestilences, famines, and natural disasters, such items will be in short supply. A wise Believer will be prepared. Being inadequately prepared does not cause Believers to lose their relation with their Lord. It just makes them foolish and places them in more sorrow than they need to experience.

There will be no running to your Christian neighbors to borrow when these days of trial come. Remember how the virgins, who ran out of oil, turned to those who had a surplus and asked if they would share it with them? The wise did not give away their precious commodity, but told the foolish virgins to go buy their own. This is not an unmerciful act of greed but one of dedication to endure until the coming of the Lord.

Questions will arise about what should one have in reserve for these days that are quickly approaching, and in what quantity? Each individual will have a unique response to these questions, for each person has different needs and aspirations. Some can live on less while others require excess.

The importance of having a Preparedness Plan remains essential to physical survival during uncertain times. Such a plan needs to include a Physical Survival Pack(s). PSP's consists of essential commodities which are needed to sustain life at a reasonable level of quality and dignity. By examining the uses of oil within the Bible, a check list can be developed to assist in the development of your own PSP. A wise Believer will be prepared. Foolish Believers get excited but at midnight will be left in the dark, unprepared.

Chapter 5

Physical Survival Pack (PSP)

❧

Five Commodities for Physical Survival

Now that we have established olive oil as a basic commodity for physical survival and discovered its uses within Scripture, we find that it provides an outline which advocates those items which can assist in creating a Physical Survival Pack (PSP). Using the example of the olive oil which was used in the parable concerning the ten virgins we discover five basic areas which a PSP should include:

- **Energy/Light source**
- **Medical supplies**
- **Hygiene/Sanitation provision**
- **Equipment and Gear**
- **Food supplies.**

The lists of equipment and supplies which follow are not inclusive but serve as a guide to begin making preparations for physical survival readiness. Failure to prepare even a modest plan for their physical survival reveals the foolishness that has caused so many Believers to miss out on the purpose which God planned for their lives. They expect God to fulfill His purpose in their lives without any preparations on their part. It reminds me of the story of a deacon that was caught in a flood somewhere in the Tennessee Valley. When the waters rose over the road in front of his house the National Guard came by in a duce-and-a-half truck to take him to safety. The deacon very piously replied that he depended upon the Lord and not the National Guard. He would just wait.

The next morning the waters were up to his front porch. A boat from the Volunteer Fire and Rescue came by and told him to climb in but again the deacon sanctimoniously responded that his hope was in the Lord and not a bunch of volunteers.

Later that evening the flood waters forced the now concerned deacon to the roof of his house. A helicopter from the Coast Guard hovered over him. After letting down a rescue basket, the deacon, though more nervous than before, reconfirmed his snobbishness by telling the fly boys that he would remain faithful and wait upon the Lord to deliver him.

That night the deacon drowned and woke up in heaven. He was so upset that he demanded to see the Lord immediately. St. Peter accommodated him and before he realized it, the deacon was standing before the Lord.

The deacon said, "I don't understand. I was faithful to you until the end waiting for your deliverance from the flood. Why did you let me drown?"

"What do you mean, 'let you drown?' I sent a truck, a boat, and a helicopter. You were too spiritual to see how practical I am when it comes to deliverance."

Don't be like the deacon in the story who thought that being practical conflicted with being spiritual. Be pragmatic and develop a Personal Survival Plan. Begin by creating your own **Physical Survival Pack**. The following suggestions can help you as you prepare.

1. Energy/Light Source:

Throughout the Bible, olive oil remained the main source for personal illumination. Such was the case in the parable in Matthew 25. **Physical Survival Packs (PSP)** need to have a light source. Much consideration and forethought should be given to how light will be provided during "Days of Sorrow" or any other disaster. From a collection of flash lights of various sizes and types, to the prospects of a generator, light sources should be a fundamental consideration.

Flash lights require batteries. Replacement batteries should be stored in quantities. Batteries often go bad and begin to leak when left in a flashlight; therefore, they should be stored in a separate container. Generators require either combustible fuels or wind. Each creates a unique problem for storage, handling and placement. Solar panels which can charge batteries can be purchased at many local stores and should be kept in mind. Small hand-crank or shake-to-shine flashlights can be found in most hardware outlets. Some of the crank-type flashlights also have radios incorporated into the device which makes it very helpful in keeping in touch with civil defense and disaster-related announcements. An emergency weather radio is also a necessary part of any **PSP**.

Radios and other communication devices fall under the **PSP** Light Source responsibility. Staying informed of the events around you in times of crisis is of utmost importance. Again, a power source to operate these items should be carefully considered. Cell phones most likely will not work due to the loss of power to the transmission towers as well as damage to the towers themselves. Two-way radios might be considered for short ranges but usually not over 5 miles. Short-wave radios are available but require a license to operate.

During times of crisis, communication can be reduced to only a sign hung up in a window or a painted message on the roof. Writing materials should be included with this segment of the **PSP**. Pencils, pens, felt markers (permanent), and cans of spray paint need to be included. Paper, poster board, packaging tape, and of course, duct tape are important items. As part of the communication package be sure to include written instructions so that all who have access to your **PSP** will be able to continue to function in case you are immobilized. Do not consider anything too small or simple for written instructions.

Give location of objects and describe usage. Write it out!

Have a spiral notebook or binder in which to keep a diary of events and to track the consumption of your resources. Books and magazines which give instruction in the areas of survival need to be readily available. Include pleasure reading material as well. Craft items that keep idle hands busy such as coloring books, puzzles, board games, and needlework provide resources to pass time when confinement to one area becomes necessary. Such activities will stimulate the mind and keep the individual alert. Lighting for reading and craft areas needs to be more than a flashlight. Lanterns which operate on oil, gas, or batteries usually provide adequate lighting for such activities.

2. Medical Supplies

Olive oil's healing properties and its use as a medicine is well documented within Scripture. Luke 10:34 records the parable of the Good Samaritan who poured oil into the cuts of the robbed and wounded traveler. Olive oil's therapeutic qualities give validation for the consideration of medical supplies as apart of any **PSP**. Healing comes from the Lord, but He has also given us the herbs of the field for our infirmities and clear teachings concerning purification.

Prescription drugs, over-the-counter medicines, and general medical supplies should be included in any **PSP**. Storing a surplus of prescription medicines must be handled with extreme care. Some prescriptions have a very short shelf life and cannot be stored for a prolonged period of time. Developing a rotation schedule will keep prescriptions fresh and effective. Ask your physician for trial packets of your prescriptions. This will help establish a surplus without creating financial difficulties. Inform your physician about the **PSP** surplus you are establishing. He may have other items that he might contribute.

Most over-the-counter products have a shelf life and need to be kept fresh as well. Packaging dates are helpful in establishing usefulness, but many over the counter products will last for a long time if they are kept in an air tight container, out of sun light, and away from extreme temperatures. Pamphlets or books about natural cures or one which discusses alternative medicines might prove to be helpful.

General first aid supplies such as bandages, sterile gauze, tape, cotton swabs, and disinfectants should be in ample supply. Hydrogen peroxide is a good purification agent and is very inexpensive. Non-latex gloves, surgical masks, antiseptic wipes, and alcohol-based hand sanitizer needs to be in a quantity that would meet the need of the number of persons being served by the **PSP**. During times of disasters, First Aid often ends up as long term care; prepare accordingly. The **PSP** medical supplies should be clearly marked and in a central location.

3. Hygiene/Sanitation Provisions

Olive oil also found use in Biblical time as a commodity for personal hygiene. In Psalm 104:15, oil was used to make the face to shine. The 23rd Psalm, reads "he anointed my head with oil." Personal hygiene, even during times of emergency and disasters, must be a major consideration for inclusion into the **PSP**. Hygiene articles for bathing, washing clothes, and the cleaning of the living environment are essential to the over all health of all who are being served by the **PSP**. Toilet paper, paper towels, napkins and feminine supplies fall within this section of the **PSP**. Clothing and bedding need to be well planned. Consider all weather aspects in these preparations. Long sleeves can be rolled up but short sleeves cannot be rolled down. Remember, clothes need to be washed and often decontaminated so include the proper cleansing products. Soap and detergents must be included. Hand soap, waterless hand cleaners and bleach are a necessity. Paper and cloth towels will be required for hand washing and general bathing. Take careful consideration about what may be used for washbasins and sterilization stations. These containers can serve as storage containers until they are need.

Garbage removal and disposal must be careful considered. Plastic bags serve only as a temporary solution. Garbage should be incinerated when possible or buried within twenty-four hours to eliminate disease. Make preparations also for human waste disposal.

4. Equipment and Gear

The oil in the parable of the ten virgins was put into lamps. These clay lamps made the oil useful. This demonstrates the importance of equipment and gear in the development of the **PSP**. This section of your **Personal Survival Pack** covers a vast assortment of resources of food preparation items, shelter, tools, gardening utensils and items of personal defense or protection.

Cooking, in some cases, will be very difficult. If a generator is available, the task is somewhat easier. A two burner hot plate will provide adequate heat for cooking. However, there is no assurance that it will be usable for a long period of time. Other means of cooking should be explored and included in the **PSP**. Bottled propane or gel heat provide reliable alternatives. Propane cook stoves or other types of gas stoves are available, but again require a stockpile of fuel. They also give off a considerable amount of carbon monoxide and should not be used in an enclosed area. Fuel canisters should never be stored in the living environment. Wood stoves, sometimes, are a feasible alternative if smoke removal is available.

No matter how the food is cooked, it has to be placed in pots, on plates and served with eating utensils. Both hot and cold drinking containers will be required. Disposable dishes and utensils take care of the cleaning problem but create a trash crisis. The storage of paper products also causes a problem considering the number of items that will be needed over a long period of time. Although paper products are useful, they should not be the only consideration. Basic food preparation tools such as knives, hand mixers, ladles, pots and pans, gallon jars, wash pots, and containers for both potable and non-potable water should be included in the **PSP**.

5. Food Supply

Last, but not least, is food. Olive oil as a food source is found in both the Old and New Testaments. It was used in baking, frying and boiling. In Revelation 6:6 we read that the angel was told not to hurt the oil or the wine. Both of these items have very long shelf life and can be kept for extended periods of time. People often put up food without much consideration as to the shelf life and the durability of a product. First consideration in the storing of food should be given to those products which have not been precooked and are in a dried or dehydrated condition, such as beans and rice. Dehydrated products such as noodles, potatoes and meats have a long shelf life. Canned products or air tight packaging can be stored for long periods of time but remember that the animals and insects will be hungry too, so products that are packaged in foil or paper need to be placed in glass jars for protection. All food needs to be rotated so the shelf life is maximized. Once you have established your supplies, be sure to keep a record of their shelf life and keep the freshest products in your storage area.

Including a few packages of vegetable seeds for planting would be prudent. Freezing the seeds helps preserve their efficiency for several years; however, once taken out of the freezer, they need to be placed in an air-tight metal or glass container or, if possible, planted immediately Remember to harvest seeds from your garden for planting the next season.

Frozen foods should be given the least consideration as a food source for a **PSP** because of the unpredictability of public utilities and the inefficiency of generators. If you have a supply of frozen food at the beginning of a disaster or emergency be sure to cook or use it first. Consider smoking or grilling all frozen meats immediately. This will maintain their usefulness as a food source for several days or even weeks. Some meats can be turned into jerky and last even longer.

Water requirements remain a key element in human survival. It takes a lot of water to prepare food, for consumption, and for hygiene usages. Most experts suggest storing a minimum of one gallon per day per person in the **PSP** group. This however is only a minimum consideration. Water purification tablets or other water purification techniques need to be a part of the food supply. Carbonated drinks are not advisable for **PSP.**

Even though many Christians do not partake in the consumption of any alcohol product, prayerful consideration should be made in the use of wine as a part of any **PSP.** Wine's health-giving qualities remain undisputed and are substantiated in scripture (1 Timothy 5:23). It is also a purification agent and aids in the preparations of food.

What should be the duration
period of a PSP?

Again let us go to the Bible for help as to how long one should rely upon a PSP for survival. The oil lamps used by the Virgins were normally good for one to three hours. In other words, their lamps would have gone out somewhere around 10 or 11 o'clock. There came a cry at midnight that the bridegroom was coming. They woke up and lit their lamps. Notice, the cry was not that the bridegroom was there but only that he was coming. They were not told how long it would take the bridegroom to get to where they were, only that he was getting close.

No one knows the day or the hour the Son of Man will come. Only the Father knows when Jesus will return to earth. However, according to Jesus, we will know the signs of the time of His coming. He said that man can discern the weather by watching the sky. Evening and morning are the times given during which the weather can be predicted with some accuracy. Both segments consist of a time period of approximately three hours. Jesus said in Acts 1:7 that we do not know the season but such information tells us that it will be in one of the seasons of the earth. Seasons are divided into 3 month segments: summer, spring, winter and fall. Three hours of light, three months of a season and three years of worldly ministry of Jesus. There seems to be a pattern here but which one should be used as a guide to stock a PSP?

Some use the three year pattern in storing supplies. Others store provisions for seven years. However, this creates a great concern for maintaining shelf life for some foods and the rotation requirements for prescription medicines. Keeping a **PSP** that would last a year or more creates a great logistic problem. The parable about the virgins suggest only a few hours of reserves which seems insufficient as a duration period for a **PSP**. A reasonable length for a **PSP** to be used appears to be three months. This in no way suggests that a **PSP** should be limited only to three months. Three months should be only a minimum.

Another reason for having supplies for three months is that this would provide a safe period of time to recover from a natural disaster, a pandemic or biological terrorism. In the case of nuclear fallout, three month quarantine would be a minimum time for decontamination, depending upon one's location in relation to the ignition area. Supplies less than three months would not provide adequate provisions.

In a natural disaster like a hurricane, a three month supply of recourses can be inadequate. After hurricane Rita in 2005, it took many people of Southwest Louisiana and Southeast Texas more than three months to return to normalcy. For some, it took longer than that. It took years for some people in New Orleans get their homes back in living order after hurricane Katrina. Although a three month supply of food and medicines would have been inadequate in the long run, it would have been a stop-gap until the national aid arrived.

Likewise, a pandemic takes from six to eight weeks to complete a full disease cycle but even at that, mutations can linger a few weeks longer. In nuclear fallout, large contaminated objects take a longer time to reach levels tolerable for human exposure. Smaller particles dissipate more rapidly. There is concern, however, that with a dirty bomb, because it is a conventional explosion that scatters radioactive material, that contamination period will be longer than that of a nuclear bomb. A dirty bomb can leave an area radioactive for years. The upside to all this it is that the area contaminated by a dirty bomb will be smaller than that of a conventional nuclear blast. However, such a bomb could interrupt commerce and business in the targeted area for very long periods of time. This would cause havoc for months over other parts of the nation as well.

Having a PSP which will last for at least three months remains a basic requirement for survival times of disaster. To plan for less would be like the five foolish virgins who ran out of oil at midnight. Remember, three months remains the minimum duration period for a **PSP.**

Why would anyone want to be prepared and ready? First, being prepared is just smart. Second, it is what the Bible teaches. Rapture-based theology has caused some Believers to stop their preparations for they see no need to prepare. Such an error will cause much sorrow. Rapture or not, Believers must be prepared to endure the "Days of Sorrow." Be prepared!

Chapter 6

Eternal/Spiritual Preparedness (ESP)

❧

As we have observed earlier, the human experience finds expression in three areas of awareness: Body, Mind and Soul. Even though Christianity embraces all three areas through its doctrine, duty, and devotion, the post-modern mind-set seemingly restricts religion to only the spiritual element of the soul. Post-modern thinkers contend that the Church should restrict its influence and authority to the spiritual arena and stay out of the physical or mental areas of the human experience. Evidence of such an attitude can readily be noted in the crisis management response manuals and disaster planning manuals found in government and industrial institutions. Spiritual concerns seldom appear on any of the pre-disaster check lists. If they do, it is an afterthought; if it is a thought at all.

Contrary to the consensus of the post-modern majority, the Word of God does address the whole man. To endure to the end requires that there be spiritual preparedness as well as physical preparation. In His teachings, found in Matthew 25, Jesus uses a parable to illustrate that this preparation for His Second Coming must include more than mere physical readiness.

In this parable Jesus emphasizes the importance of being spiritually prepared for His return. Often called the "Parable of the Unprofitable Servant," this parable speaks of a wealthy man who made plans to take an extended trip into a far country. Before he left he called in his **OWN** servants and transferred unto them a portion of his wealth. To one servant he entrusted five talents. To the next servant he assigned two talents. To the third servant he allocated only one talent. Then the master left immediately upon his journey.

Jesus said that the servant who received the five talents went out and invested his share and earned five more. The servant who accepted the two talents did likewise and he too doubled what had been allotted him. However, the servant who received the one talent was so driven by his own fears of inadequacies that he went out and hid the talent in the ground. He feared he would do something wrong and lose the investment. He feared taking a risk. Undoubtedly, to him, venturing out into a new area of faith provided too many opportunities for failure. What he truly did not fear was his master. If he had, he would have at least put the capital into some type of minimum, secured investment. Although the proceeds would have been small, he would have shown an increase.

Jesus then drew attention to the fact that after a long period of time the master returned. In emphasizing the length of the journey the master took, Jesus communicated precisely that the man was not after a short term windfall-profit, but was interested in long term investments.

If you have not yet noticed, God is a long-term investor. Short-term investments fluctuate too much for any substantial gain. Like any other long-term investor, the Lord knows that there will be ups and downs in the spiritual market of our lives. However, the portfolio which is dedicated to the long-term strategy will, in the end, have a greater increase in value.

As in any long-term investment strategy, gains and losses occur but the overall long-term performance remains the target of the wise investor. Many Believers seem to be looking for those spiritual opportunities that offer quick windfall return, but if this parable teaches anything, it is that the Lord is interested in "long-term performance." Quick gains within spiritual portfolios usually evaporate before they can be cashed out. This philosophy of long-term performance finds little fertile ground in the "instant gratification society" of the post-modern world. Like day-traders of the 90's, some post-modern Believers pull out of the spiritual market at the first sign of trouble. Cashing out too early can reduce the portfolio's overall spiritual results.

From this parable we learn that the two servants, who were willing to keep the endowments active in the market, doubled what they had been allotted. Fearing he might lose what he had been given because of his own inabilities, the servant who had received the one talent buried his portion in the ground. To him, taking the path of least risk was the best risk to take. That concept failed not only him, but his master as well.

Upon his return the master called in his servants for evaluation. The two servants, who kept their master's assets in the market, double the value of the talents which had been entrusted to them. Both were called "**good and faithful**." Both were praised and rewarded even though the amounts of their gains were different. The master did not differentiate between the two because of the monetary amounts but rewarded them equally. They received the same rewards because it took a comparable amount of risk from each servant to obtain the same percentage of increase.

Being honored by receiving the title "good and faithful" was not the only reward these two servants enjoyed. They both received more responsibility with greater opportunities. They were promoted from servants to rulers. But that is still not all. In verse 28, the master instructs his accountant to take the one talent from the servant who failed to do anything and give it to the one who doubled his five. Notice that the master referred to that servant not as the one, "who **had** ten" but rather "who **has** ten." The master had left the initial investment and the increase with the faithful servants. In other words, for the time the master was gone, the two who were working for their lord actually ended up working for themselves. They were laying up treasures for themselves by increasing what had been entrusted to them by their master.

Jesus says in Matthew 6:19, "Lay not up for yourselves treasures upon earth, where moth and rust doth corrupt, and where thieves break through and steal: but lay up for yourselves treasures in heaven, where neither moth nor rust doth corrupt, and where thieves do not break through nor steal: for where your treasure is there will your heart be also." It is obvious that, although monetary assessment does not characterize spiritual reward, it is incorporated in its concept.

The servant who hid his talent suffered an entirely different conclusion for his lack of effort. He had carefully planned a speech to defend his decision for not investing his resources as had his fellow servants. His explanation, however, failed to impress the master. In fact, the master used the servant's own words as an indictment against him. The wasteful servant received no honor or praise as did his two fellow servants. Instead, this poor fellow was humiliated by his master when he was labeled as "wicked and slothful."

These two terms conjure up images of evil and slothfulness. A little understanding of the syntax of words can reveal a fuller understanding of the scripture. The term slothful has, for the most part, lost its significance within the post-modern English language. The term translates better as lazy or obtuse. The original Greek word could also be translated as tardy, indicating a purposed desire to lay back or be hesitant in making a decision. Lazy indicated a lack of thought, projecting a passive approach to any given situation. This servant was not passive, but made a decision to be cautious. He did not want to get involved in the nitty-gritty of investing his master's talent. He chose to play it safe and came up short. The term "tardy" implicates slowness as in ones inability to think rationally. The word "retarded" reflects this meaning. Bluntly put, being tardy is being dim-witted. Think about that the next time you are late for a meeting.

If embarrassment had been his only punishment, the foolish servant might have endured the shame, but his master was not about to stop there. After stripping the fearful servant of any integrity, the master then took away his talent and gave it to someone else. After labeling him an unprofitable servant, the master had him forcefully removed from his presence and "cast into outer darkness where there was weeping and gnashing of teeth."

For the most part, post-modern Believers find little value in this parable. They have been convinced that its teaching has nothing to do with them or with the kingdom of Heaven. Because of their feel-good theology, they are convinced that Heaven is a happy and glorious place, free of any negative vibes. They sing of "no tears up there," so surely there is no weeping or gnashing of teeth in the eternal utopia.

Certainly, they believe, this must address the lost souls, but surely not the Redeemed.

What about Revelation 22:15, which reads, "Outside the city are the dogs, the sorcerers, the sexually immoral, the murderers, the idol worshipers, and all who love to live a lie." "Outside what city?" one may ask. It is none other than the New Jerusalem which comes down out of heaven and is suspended between heaven and earth at the beginning of the Millennium reign of Christ. This is the celestial city which Jesus told His disciples about just before His death. This is the place where there are many rooms. In this city, the New Jerusalem, Jesus will be the Light, and there the Tree of Life will grow, and the River of Waters will flow. John tells us that not everyone will be allowed into that city, for only those who are written in the Lamb's Book of Life will be allow into the city. We are told that those who are not found in the Book of Life are cast into the lake of fire (20:15), so, there appears to be a group of souls, found in the Book of Life but not in the Lamb's Book of Life. Who are these people who are not given access to the city? Could this be the unfaithful servants who escape hell by the Blood of the Lamb but not the eternal chastisement of God? Are these the unprofitable servants who are not allowed into the Holy City? Are they destined to eat the crumbs that fall from the master's table (Matthew 15:27)?

Why would an unfaithful servant expect more than crumbs to begin with? The Blood of Jesus saves the fallen soul from the torment of Hell but not from the chastisement of God. The Bible tells us that "those whom He loves He chastises." Lest you forget, it is a "terrible thing to fall into the hands of the living God." How easy it is to ignore scriptures that do not fit our theology. Ignoring selected verses is the intellectual's deceptive way of excluding them.

The Gospel of Luke presents another parable about a nobleman who had ten servants. He divided his wealth among them. On his return the noble called in all his servants to give an account of their handling of his money. The outcome of this parable is very similar to the one in Matthew. The servants in that passage who increased what they had been given were rewarded, but the one who did nothing was punished.

When defining an unprofitable servant, Jesus added His usual straight-forward clarification. Most would assume that an unjust or unprofitable servant would be one who would waste his master's substance, embezzle his assets, or fail to perform the work assigned. Jesus saw it in a completely different context. His evaluation of an unprofitable servant might be the most condemning and uncompromising definition in all of scripture. In Luke 17:10 Jesus identifies and describes an unprofitable servant. He says, "...so likewise ye, when you shall have done all those things which are commanded you, say, 'we are **unprofitable servants**: we have done that which was our duty to do' (emphasis added)." This verse clearly teaches that doing only what is required amounts to no more than performing what would be considered by the Lord as a minimum response. A life of minimum spiritual service falls short of a life worthy of reward. In fact, Jesus calls the minimum Believer, "Unfaithful."

How many Church members are really spiritually ready for the coming of Jesus? How many Christians are sincerely ready for the "Days of Sorrow" and the pending scrutiny of the Judgment Seat of Christ? Comments like, "I've been baptized," "I joined the church," "I raised my kids in Sunday School," "I paid my tithes," "I read my Bible," or "I prayed," are minimum performances of one's spiritual duty for which they will never hear, "Well done thou good and faithful servant." According to scripture, a Believer who does only what is required is classified as an unprofitable servant and will receive for his efforts, that which is allotted to the hypocrite. A servant who does only the minimum is not only unprofitable, but according to the teachings of Jesus is evil and lazy (dim-witted).

Consider the servant who was given the one talent, and hid it in the ground so he wouldn't lose it. When his master returned, the servant was able to give back exactly what had been given, but that was not the purpose of being entrusted with the money. In Matthew 5:15, Jesus said, "...neither do men light a candle and put it under a bushel, but on a candlestick; and it giveth light unto all that are in the house. Let your light so shine before men that they may see your good works and glorify your Father which is in heaven." The gifts of God are not given to be hidden behind stained glass windows but are to be thrown into the market place of everyday living. Yes, it is risky, but it is the only way a spiritual portfolio can grow in value.

The church has been satisfied much too long with simply "having the Light" when Jesus' purpose in giving the Light was for the Church to become the Light. That purpose will not be realized through minimum Christian service.

Jesus says that those who have the light of the Holy Spirit in them are the "light of the world" and they are to let their "light shine before men." This is expected of each Christian. To become a light, which can not be hidden, sitting upon a hill is still the minimum service required of each disciple of Christ.

Jesus told his Disciples to "store up treasure in heaven." Minimum service offers no treasure. Failing to take the risk of faith leaves the follower of Christ spiritually bankrupt. To prosper from the quarry of faith, there has to be elements of risk. It is high upon the slippery slopes of faith where the blessings of God are found. There on the steep, ragged crevasses of faith, is where weary believers find nuggets of heaven's purest treasure. To have treasures in heaven Christians must stop prospecting in the valleys of comfort and risk all for the Glory of God, high upon the mountain of faith.

It is true that some treasure can be found in the valley, but here is where Christians are to discover the smooth stones needed to face the giants of life. If it is abundant treasure they seek, they must walk out of the valley and climb into the mountains. Too many have settled for a few specks of eternal treasure panned out of the river of life, when there, upon the mountain of faith, lies the mother load of eternal reward. Hidden within the depths of adversity and risk, the vein of heaven's purest gold can be found. Go for it! Jesus promises that, "He that seeks shall find...."

He also said, in John 15:8, that the Father is glorified when we produce much spiritual fruit. We might be satisfied with a small bag of gold from the foot-hills of faith, but God receives glory when we hit the ore bed of divine grace and mine from its wealth, not bags, but train loads of heaven's treasure. We have not been called to be minimum Believers but rather, radical witnesses of the grace of God.

The Lord makes this very clear. He does not suggest, but rather commands, His servants to produce much fruit. Minimum productions produce maximum chastisement. Luke 12:47 should send shivers of shame down the backs of most Christians. It reads, "...And that servant, which knew his lord's will and **prepared not himself**, neither did according to his will, shall be beaten with many stripes (emphasis added)."

Jesus began His discussion in Luke 12:42-48 by asking the question, "Who then is that **faithful** and **wise** steward, whom his lord **shall** make ruler over his household, to give **them their portion of meat** in due season?" Here the scripture sheds some insightful knowledge upon the different degrees of the eternal experience and reward.

The Blood of Jesus saves the soul from eternal punishment but not from the chastening of the Lord.

Paul writes in 1 Corinthians 11:32 that "...when we are judged, we are chastened of the Lord, that we should not be condemned with the world". Our service (works) has no effect upon the work which the Blood of Christ has accomplished, but it does have an effect upon our heavenly experience.

Returning to the parable found in Matthew 25:14-30, we find that again the Lord lays out a vivid strategy to follow in preparing ourselves for the perilous days ahead. In the next chapter we will look more closely at this outline while considering the importance of spiritual preparedness as we approach the coming of the Lord. But before you turn the page, spend a moment in prayer and meditation. Ask yourself if you are a minimum Believer or are you a Spiritual Mountain Climber? It is not too late to learn to climb.

Many scriptures underline the importance of Eternal Spiritual Preparedness as the day of the Lord's return draws near. Matthew 12:36 warns that "every idle word that men shall speak, they shall give account thereof in the day of judgment." Everyone, Believers and non-believers alike, will give an account of their life in all three areas: body, mind, and soul. Romans 14:12 confirms that "...every one of us shall give account of himself to God." Luke 12:48 speaks directly to the Church of the twenty-first century by saying, "...Unto whomsoever much is given, of him shall be much required." Without question, Americans fall under the category of "whomsoever much has been given." This nation has been given much, therefore, much will be required.

Do not be confused between being saved and being prepared. As paradoxical as it may sound, there will be many who are saved by the Blood of Jesus who are not spiritually ready for His Return. The question is, are you?

_____ **Chapter** ⟨ 7 ⟩

MUCH IS GIVEN...
MUCH REQUIRED

❧

B elow are five proven growth strategies taken from Matthew 25:14-30, which, if adhered to, will allow even the most modest of divine-gifts portfolio to grow within the spiritual marketplace. Although these strategies will undoubtedly have some variances and risks that will often appear to show losses, the overwhelming results in following these strategies will amount to long-term gain. Jesus did not die on the cross so the Redeemed could just sit back and cruise into eternity on a low risk 401-K plan. He set us free from the bondage of sin and shame so we could take great leaps of faith in the market-place of eternal dimension. When Jesus returns, He will require each Believer to give a full disclosure of his spiritual portfolio. Now is the time to invest. Now is the time to prepare for the divine audit. It is time to invest ourselves into God's marketplace. Here is how this can be done:

1. Become a servant of the Living God.

The first thing that should be noticed in this parable is that only those servants who belonged to the master were given investments. Not servants in general but his **own** servants. These men were bond-servants, men who had freely given themselves to the will of the master. They had been bought with a price. They were not their own. This is a very important fact that must be understood. The first step of spiritual preparedness is accepting Jesus as Lord.

The old debate continues as to whether or not a man can accept Jesus as Savior without making him Lord. Nevertheless, many give verbal witness that Jesus is their Savior but by the way they live their lives He definitely is not their Lord. They readily claim Jesus as Savior but live their lives in response to their own ambitions and desires. They pray and do all sorts of religious activities but all this activity is motivated by selfish ambitions and thirst for power. Jesus rejected these religious activists in Matthew 7:21-23, saying, "...depart from me... I never knew you."

In other words these activists observed religious things but thought only about themselves. They truly had not dedicated themselves to the Lord and His kingdom. They failed to put His interests and desires ahead of their own. Jesus addressed this behavior in Luke 16: 13, when He said, "No servant can serve two masters: for either he will hate the one and love the other; or else he will hold to the one, and despise the other. Ye cannot serve God and Mammon." In other words, a man cannot serve his own selfish interests, i.e., wealth and possessions, and God at the same time.

Far too many Believers today consider Jesus to be the servant and themselves the master. Through religious activities and practices, they dictate what He must accomplish for them. By pointing to their minimum activities, they seek to manipulate Him into doing work for their own personal interest, rather than for His Kingdom. What happened to that part of the model prayer that reads, "Thy kingdom come, thy will be done?"

Jesus makes it very clear that those servants found doing something other than that they were instructed to do will be beaten with many stripes. Should we discuss the words, "beat and stripes"? Is there any question to the fact that at the coming of the Lord many, many Believers will be weeping and wailing?

The first requirement in being prepared spiritually for the Lord's return is to commit to His Lordship over your life. Surrender your will and fears. Release your doubt about your own abilities and rest assuredly upon His faithfulness. He who has called you will finish what He has begun. Place yourself in the center of His will and do not fear failure. The only failure you need to fear is failing to make Him your Lord.

2. Invest all spiritual assets.

The next significant principle found in this parable is that, the master did not randomly distribute his investments. He gave according to their individual abilities. The Lord desires success and not failure. He will not put more on His servants than that which they can carry. However, when He does give out assets of spiritual value, He requires much increase.

The logical man, with all his cautiousness and calculations cannot produce the growth that the Lord requires. Only faith can produce the returns that give glory to the Father. This is not a faith in faith concept but rather a commitment to the three aspects of eternal investment.

First, there must be a faith in the Father and His purpose for our lives. Second, faith must be placed in the fact that the gift itself was given to us by the Father of all wisdom, who above all knows our potential. Last, faith must be placed in the spiritual market place in which our gifts will be invested. Without this type of faith, there will be no spiritual gain or reward.

Because faith fails to be a part of their investment strategy, many Believers, like the unprofitable servant, accomplish nothing. Their cautiousness and timidity reveal a complete lack of trust for the Lord's purpose and plan for their lives. The Bible clearly teaches that whatever is not of faith is sin. Therefore, not investing or taking risks with your spiritual gift is a sin.

It must be remembered that the evaluation of personal worth by God does not follow the greedy assessment of man, which focuses solely upon the valued measurement of gain. Everyone has heard, "He who dies with the most toys, wins." A silly statement, but sadly many people live by this axiom. Do not forget that the Lord, too, is interested in gains; however, it is the gain within the soul He seeks.

Each Believer has received a spiritual gift by which he can enhance the Church. These spiritual gifts are not ours but belong to the Lord. They are not to be used for any personal gain or for fulfillment of some selfish spiritual satisfaction, but rather for the will and purposes of God and His Kingdom. In 1 Peter 4:10 we read, "Every man hath received the gift, even so minister the same one to another, as good stewards of the manifold grace of God." Paul says, in 1 Corinthians 12:7, "But the manifestation of the Spirit is given to every man to the profit withal."

Remember that the spiritual gift you hold is not your possession. It belongs to the Lord. He has entrusted it to your keeping for increase. You are to use it and increase it for His good.

There is an old saying that goes, "Use it or lose it." How truly that resounds within the spiritual framework of gifts. Many may have lost their spiritual giftedness; they have failed to do anything with it because they are afraid of failure or embarrassment. They choose the easy way out and discover the hard reality of their slothfulness.

Where no risk is involved, faith is not required. Without faith, works are dead. In other words, nothing happens. To be spiritually ready for the Lord's return means that we must, by faith, invest our spiritual gift-edness into the busy marketplace of service. It is true we might fail. However, we get up and try again, and again, and again until we succeed. If you are trying, you are preparing.

3. Take Spiritual Risk

The two servants who received the more size-able amounts of money risked it all by placing it in the market. After a while, they both showed an increase. We do not know how much each lost during the investment period, but one thing we do know; they eventually increased their holdings. With every investment, whether in the marketplace of ideas, of finances, or of faith, there is a potential of setbacks. However, a basic axiom of investment is, "the greater the likelihood of loss, the greater the potential of gain." This holds true with any investment, but in the marketplace of divine purpose there is another undisputable truth that takes some of the sting out of what we might see as a potential spiritual deficit. This truth says: "All things work together for good for those who love the Lord and are called according to his purpose."

When will Christians wake up and realize that with the Lord it is a win-win situation? Even when we lose, we win. In fact, the only way to lose is do nothing. Only when we fail to step out in faith do we lose.

Did Peter lose when he stepped out of the boat? "But he sank," you say. Did he? All we know is that he began to sink. He is the only man to have walked on water other than the Lord. Sounds like a winner to me! Remember when Moses had to pick up the snake by the tail? Remember when Gideon had to attack an army with only 300 men? What about David facing the giant with five smooth stones. They all took risks. Walking with God is risky business, but has the best guarantee there is: "...with God all things are possible."

When it comes to faith, the risk most Believers have trouble taking does not lie within the realm of spiritual substance but in the area of physical consideration. Here they have a hard time trusting God with their physical well being. They have a hard time exercising faith when it comes to risky situations? They trust Him with their souls but they fail to trust Him with their day to day existence?

Faith is not about what you confess. Talk is cheap. Paul said that you would know his faith by his works. This is the type of faith in which "the rubber meets the road." It is a faith which is not talked about, but is lived out in every aspect of life.

What the Master looks for in servants is faithfulness. He is not listening to what they say; rather, He is watching what they do. His judgments rest on their actions. How they live reveals what they truly believe. If they believe God is powerless in their physical life to protect or provide, they will bury what little spirituality they have in fear of losing it, too. On the other hand, where faith in God abounds, servants take considerable amounts of risk. In so doing, they bring great glory to the Father through their spiritual investments.

Jesus points out this fact, in Luke 18:8, when he asks the rhetorical question, "Nevertheless, when the Son of man cometh, shall he find faith on the earth?" Will he find you living by faith or living in fear? To be spiritually prepared for the coming of the Lord will result in the abandonment of physical securities for lucrative spiritual gains of faith.

4. Be prepared for an audit at all times.

Very few investors look forward to an audit by the IRS, but such a scenario gives a good analogy of what will happen at the Bema-Seat Judgment. The eternal audit of a Believer's spiritual portfolio is called the Judgment Seat of Christ. At this spiritual audit Believers from all eras of history will have their lives evaluated. This is not a place where judgment is passed upon one's salvation; rather it is an evaluation of works or the lack thereof. To this end Paul writes in Philippians 2:12, "...work out your own salvation with fear and trembling. For it is God which worketh in you both to will and to do of his good pleasure."

What has happened to the fear and trembling among Believers concerning the way they live their lives? Does anyone fears the Lord any more? It seems that the message about the Grace and Mercy of God has immunized the redeemed soul from fear. Or has the post-modern church confused guilt with legitimate fear?

Concerning the final evaluation of the Christian's job performance, Paul writes in Romans 14:12, "So then every one of us shall give account (evaluation) of himself to God." Jesus makes an even more profound statement by saying that "...every idle word that men shall speak, they shall give account thereof in the day of judgment. For by thy words (*logos*-works) thou shalt be justified, and by thy words (*logos*-works) thou shalt be condemned(Matthew 12:36-37)."

"Logos," the Greek word used here by Christ to identify that which will condemn or justify a person, must not be taken lightly. Its usage suggests a physical action. The word *"logos"* describes something that has been manifested as in an act or a deed. The *"logos"* often refers to the written word of God, whereas *"rhema"* identifies the spoken word. If Jesus was speaking exclusively about speech, he would have not used the word *"logos."*

Again in Matthew 15:11, Jesus teaches the power of one's words (*logos*), upon their judgment: "Not that which goeth into the mouth defileth a man; but that which cometh out of the mouth, this defileth a man."

Without question this verse is not a reference concerning spiritual regurgitation; it concerns the deeds of man which find motivation within his heart. Jesus was speaking to people who put a lot of emphasis upon outward appearances, but had no fear of the Lord concerning their inward meditations.

Salvation of the soul from Hell remains the ultimate gift of God through the Blood of Jesus, who paid the redemptive price of man's fallen state. This

Divine audit at the Judgment Seat of Christ, which evaluates the performance and productivity of the soul, focuses firmly upon the freewill of the individual. The Lord does not force anyone to walk on streets of gold nor to serve in close proximity to His throne. These choices remain with each believer. The evaluation one receives at the judgment seat of Christ will determine the substance of his eternal experience, not his salvation. To some the Lord will say, "Come and inherit the kingdom prepared for you," and to others he will say, "Depart from me you who work iniquity."

Matthew 24:51 and 25:30 both reveal what happens to servants who have no fear (terror) for their Master. Neither of the servants was stripped of his servanthood because of his casualness towards his Master's desires. However, as a result of the indifference to their Master's will, both did lose physically. The talents which they had been given (i.e. the gift) were stripped from them. Next, although they kept their relationship as servants, their classification changed to that of being unprofitable, and thereby losing any direct contact with their Master. They lost the presence of his face and were placed in darkness where there was heard weeping and gnashing of teeth.

For some strange reason, most post-modern Believers think that a ticket out of Hell is a guaranteed reservation at the Heavenly party. They conclude, since Hell has been avoided, that there remains no punishment to fear. In their thinking, heaven is only a place of pure bliss that awaits those who have been redeemed from the Devil's torment. But from what source does such thinking come? Surly it can not from the Word of God.

Luke 12:47 teaches that "the servant that knew his lord's will and did not prepare nor did according to his will was beaten with many stripes." This situation does not sound very blissful to me. Matthew 18:22-34 teaches another lesson concerning the Kingdom of God. It reveals a fearful fate for a servant of God who does not do the will of the Father. It reads, "And his lord was wroth, and delivered him to the tormentors, till he should pay all that was due unto him. So likewise shall my heavenly Father do also unto you, if ye from your hearts forgive not every one his brother their trespasses."

Who are these tormentors and when will this tormenting transpire? For some strange reason, postmodern Believers do not envision the God of Grace and Mercy as being wroth or upset. The scriptures, however, clearly reveal that the Lord can be provoked or infuriated.

The prophet Isaiah wrote in 65:1-3, 5, *"I am sought of them that asked not for me; I am found of them that sought me not: I said, behold me, and behold me, unto a nation that was not called by my name. I have spread out my hands all the day unto a rebellious people, which walketh in a way that is not good, after their own thoughts; **a people that provoketh me to anger continually to my face**; that sacrificeth in gardens and burnedth incense upon altars of brick;...which say, Stand by thyself, come not near to me; for I am holier than thou. These are a smoke* *in my nose, a fire that burneth all the day* (Emphasis added)."

Nothing seems to aggravate the eyes more than smoke. If you move around a camp fire, no matter where you go, it seems that the smoke follows, constantly aggravating. Isaiah states that those who follow their own reasoning and consider themselves holier than others are like an irritating fire that smolders all day, giving no relief from its nuisance. The Lord is slow to anger but the day will come when at last the smoking flax will provoke the Lord to the point where He will say that enough is enough and put the fire out, removing the aggravation from His presence. Somehow, the thought of God being aggravated but patient appears contradictory. The two concepts just do not readily go together. Nevertheless, such will be the case when He begins the evaluation of His servants.

Paul reveals in 1 Corinthians 3:13 that every man's work (*logos*) will be tried by fire. All works, whether bad or good, will be tested by the same hot, consuming fire (Hebrew 12:29). The blast from the furnace of God's righteousness will consume any and all dross that is hidden within the soul of the Believer. Nothing will be left unrevealed.

I have gone into steel mills where blast furnaces are used to melt down recyclable metals. These are not places I would recommend for vacation or places to find much rest or relaxation. Every one who works there seems to yell at each other because of the noise from the furnaces. The intense heat consumes the oxygen and the smell of sulfur and pollutants stifles breathing. It is hot, dirty, and hard work. Tons of scrap iron are dumped into the furnace and the process begins. Sometimes there are explosions in the exchange of heat. Sometimes very little useable metal emerges from the furnace because the scrap iron contained useless materials like dirt, glass, plastics and such. Rarely does the amount of scrap iron dumped into the furnace equate to the amount of useable molten metal that is poured out. Depending upon the specifications for the recycled metal, the process may go through repeated steps of additional blasting before the carbon mixture is met.

This illustrates what the Bible teaches will happen at the Bema Seat Evaluation. All will be subject to the consuming fire of God's evaluation. Paul concludes his teaching about the trial of fire in verses 14-15; "If any man's work abide which he hath built thereupon, he shall receive a **reward**. If any man's work shall be burned, he shall **suffer loss**: but he himself shall be saved; yet so as by fire (Emphasis added)."

Many times this author has heard Believers say that they didn't want any rewards in Heaven, for just being there would be reward enough in itself. Such foolish talk reveals a lack of Biblical knowledge concerning eternity. Paul in his writings gives no place for an in-between crowd which is unaffected by the judgment. He saw only two groups; those with reward and those who suffered loss. The evidence shows clearly that there are only two groups of people. As in the world today there are only those who are saved and those who are lost. There exists no in-between group called the "almost lost "or "almost saved." Likewise, at the Bema Seat Judgment there will only be two groups: those with rewards and those who suffer loss. There will not be any middle group called "the just glad to be here" gang.

Returning to the parables Jesus gave concerning the unprofitable servant, ask yourself. Do you think that the unfaithful servant, after his talent was taken and while he was being cast into darkness, was saying, "I'm just glad to be here?" I think not. If he had really feared his Master, knowing he was a just man, he would have prepared himself and his talent for his lord's return. How prepared are you?

5. Anticipate the degrees of heavenly existence.

For several years my ambition to be a farmer led me to much frustration and hard work. One of the first lessons I learned that a garden doesn't grow by itself. All the potential may be present, but the crop will not jump out of the ground by itself. Plowing, seedbed preparation, planting, watering, fertilizing, insect eradication, and harvesting: all had to be done in correct sequence to enjoy the fruit of the soil. The fact that these tasks were carried out, or the lack of attention to them had a direct correlation to the quality and quantity of the crop. If bad seed was planted, inferior crops grew, or at least tried to grow. Failure to fertilize the plants or to use insecticide stunted growth and crop production. If proper seed beds were not prepared or if drought hit the plants, little would be expected at harvest time. These simple facts about farming are not shocking to most people. They are readily understood. However, when it comes to spiritual growth and eternal harvesting of one's life it is as if these principles do not exist.

Paul teaches in Galatians 6:7, that whatsoever a man sows, that is what he will reap. In 2 Corinthians 9:6, Paul writes, "...he which sows sparingly shall reap sparingly but he who sows bountifully shall also reap bountifully." From these farming examples Paul drew spiritual significance. His first century audiences understood the clear allegory which communicated deep spiritual truths. Yet, post-modern Believers seemingly have little understanding of seed time and harvest. They approach eternity with a naive assumption that they can sow their wild oats but at harvest time count on a crop failure. Unfortunately, what we sow is what we get. How we prepare impacts what we harvest.

A Believer who sows seeds of discourse among his brethren will reap bountiful discord at judgment. The servant who takes his talent and hides them, undoubtedly sows seeds of fear, laziness, and irresponsibility. When it is time to evaluate his actions, guess what he will harvest? He will reap a bumper crop of sorrow!

In Luke 12:43 Jesus said, *"Blessed is that servant, whom his lord when he cometh shall find so doing. Of a truth I say unto you, that he will make him ruler over all that he hath. But and if that servant say in his heart, My lord delayed his coming: and shall begin to beat the menservants and maidens, and to eat and drink, and to be drunken; the lord of that servant will come in a day when he looketh not for him and* *at an hour when he is not aware, and will cut him in sunder, and will appoint him his portion with the unbelievers and that servant which knew his lord's will and **prepared not himself**, neither did according to his will shall be beaten with many stripes But he that knew not and did commit things worthy of stripes shall be beaten with few stripes. For unto whosever much is given, of him shall be much required: to whom men have committed much, of them they will ask the more* (emphasis added)."

This would be one of those texts many would love to take out of the Bible, but the reality remains. If we do not prepare as the Lord has instructed, there awaits for us a time of sorrow. All that the Lord requires is that we be prepared. He speaks to Believers not to unbelievers. To those who are Blood Bought, the Lord says, "Be prepared!" To those who know the truth and consequences of scripture are without excuse. To whom much is given much will be required. Get ready!

Chapter 8

Community Survival Awareness (CSA)

❦

As discussed in previous chapters, a fundamental difference exists between what Jesus called "the Days of Sorrow" and the events of the great tribulation which are referred to as "Jacob's troubles." Those who embrace the pre-tribulation rapture theory give little consideration to establishing a survival plan or to making any preparations for the "Days of Sorrow." Since their belief assures them that they will be taken out of this world before those dreadful things occur, they see no need to be ready to endure. Failing to consider the overwhelming probability that the church will experience the purging that has been promised in scripture could be very costly to those who are not prepared. Jesus warned those who followed Him to be prepared so that the day of His coming would not come upon them unaware.

The first step in preparing for judgment and the events that will lead up to the End of the Age begins with placing your faith in Jesus Christ as the Son of the Living God. All the physical preparations in the world amount to nothing if Jesus has not been accepted as Lord and Savior.

The Blood of Jesus cleanses the soul from the curse of sin and saves it from the Devil's Hell. But end time preparations involve more than soul readiness. They also require physical planning and watching. Preparations should be made to protect our lives as the "Days of Sorrow" quickly approach. How can we endure without taking initiatives to provide safety and protection for ourselves and our family? Though not found in the Bible, the axiom, "God helps those who help themselves" does ring with some truth.

Have you made a contingency plan in case of a disaster or terrorist attack? Have you prepared for the disruption of electricity or other utilities in case of sabotage or a storm? Are you ready for the days described by Jesus as the "Days of Sorrow"?

Our study concerning the end time events has centered on the Mt. Olive discourse of Jesus which is found in Matthew 24-25, and the parables He used to intensify His message. In His discourse, Jesus outlines three areas in which Believers should be prepared. The parable about the virgins teaches preparation in physical dimensions. The parable about the three servants, to whom were given talents, illustrates the need to be prepared spiritually. The third illustration within this trilogy teaches about the judgment of the nations and reveals the need for Community preparation. Many refer to this as the parable of the nations but really, it is not a parable at all. It is a prophecy.

Notice that Jesus uses different words in introducing each story. When He spoke about the ten virgins he said, "The kingdom of heaven is likened unto…" Here Jesus makes a comparison by saying that the kingdom was LIKE. When He shared the parable about the three servants, He said, "…the kingdom of heaven is as a man…." Here He uses an analogy to make a correlation. But when Jesus spoke of the nations, He said, "When the son of man shall come in his glory…." This is neither a metaphor nor a simile, it is **FACT!**

One of these glorious days the sky is going to roll apart like a parchment and the King of Kings and Lord of Lords will break through the boundary which separates eternity from the present and once again place his foot upon this earth. This time, however, He will be the conquering King and not a suffering Messiah. He will establish the throne of David in Jerusalem and reign a thousand years over all creation.

The world is rapidly approaching its seventh millennium. This could well be the millennium of rest, a thousand years of peace and prosperity upon planet earth. The Bible teaches that the Lord rested on the seventh day and a day to the Lord is as a thousand years.

Jesus tells us that when the Son of Man comes in His glory, He will gather all the nations for judg-

ment. But who are these people? They can not be
Believers, for as we have seen earlier, Believers have
been taken up from this world in the Rapture. Then
who are these people?

The nations remaining on the earth at the time
of the Lord's triumphant return to Jerusalem will
be the Gentile people who survived the Antichrist's
rage and who did not take the mark of the beast
or worship him. These are the same Gentiles who
endured the wrath of God when it was poured out at
the end of the great tribulation. Although the armies
of the Gentiles were destroyed in the battle for
Jerusalem in the valley of Jezreel, the population of
those nations who did not take the mark or worship
the beast will still be alive. These survivors are not
part of the redeemed because they failed to accept
Jesus as Lord and Savior. Christians will not be a part
of this congregation of people for they were raptured
before the return of Jesus. The only ones who live
on the earth at this time will be the righteous Jews
and those who didn't take the mark of the beast or
worship his image.

Those who took the mark will be cast into the
bottomless pit where the rebellious angels are kept
until the Day of Judgment. Revelation 14:9-11
reveals that whoever receives "the mark of the beast"
(666) will come under the wrath of God and be cast
into torment.

According to Scripture the surviving Gentile
nations will be divided into two groups: one placed
on the right hand of Christ and the other on the left.
To the ones on His right Jesus will say, "Come, ye

blessed of my Father, inherit the kingdom prepared for you from the foundation of the world." Jesus tells them that they are considered righteous because they have taken care of Him. When these gentiles ask why they are being extended such favor, Jesus points out all that these people have done for him. To this they ask, "When did we ever do such things for you?" Jesus tells, "If you did it to at least one of these my **brethren** you have done it unto me."

To those on His left hand Jesus says, "Depart from me you cursed into everlasting fire prepared for the devil and his angels." When they ask why, Jesus responds by giving a list of all the things they refused to do for Him. In protest they respond, "When did we do these terrible things?" Jesus replies, "Inasmuch as ye did it not to one of the least of these ye did it not to me."

To simply state it, the Gentile nations that showed mercy to the brethren of Christ will inherit the 1000 year kingdom of peace and prosperity. Those who survive the tribulation but fail to care for the brethren of Christ, even though they do not take the mark of the Antichrist, will be cast into the place of torment where the devil's angels await judgment.

But who are the brethren of Christ? The answer is simple. It is those who are of the seed of Jacob. This includes brethren of faith as well as brethren of lineage, the Jews. In Matthew 12:49, Jesus said, "...this is my mother and my brethren" in reference to the disciples, a group which, included Judas. Again at the tomb the resurrected Savior in Matthew 28: 10 tells the women to "...go tell my brethren...."

Again in John 20:17, Jesus tells Mary to "...go to my brethren." In these three cases Jesus refers to his disciples as brethren. Believers are brethren to each other and we are of the household of faith, so when we are talking about the brethren of Jesus we are referring to all the descendants of Jacob; those of Jewish-Hebrew lineage and those of faith who by the blood of Jesus have been born into the Kingdom of God.

The nations that will enjoy the millennium reign of Christ will be those who had compassion for the Jews, and the Christians before they were raptured. Those nations that did not show compassion will be cast into everlasting fire prepared for the devil and his angels.

According to Jude 6, there is a place where the fallen angels that chose to follow Satan are being held. It is called the **bottomless pit**. Revelation 9:1 tells us that from this pit smoke, like that from a great furnace, came out and darkened the sun. Revelation 20:2-3 assures us that the devil will be cast, bound in chains, into the bottomless pit for a thousand years. Revelation 20:7 reveals that Satan will be released out of this pit for a short period of time after the millennium reign.

The only people left on earth after the judgment of the nations will be those of the nation of Israel who survived the tribulation, numbering 144,000, and those of the Gentile nations that protected and aided the Jews and Christians during their suffering. This will undoubtedly leave the world with a small population, but after a thousand years of health and prosperity, the world will repopulate with millions of people. Living in a Garden-of-Eden like existence, many of these people will never know the evils of sin and its pledge upon the human soul. Generations will be born that never knew temptation or sin of any kind. However, when the devil is loosed from the pit at the end of the millennium, he will tempt them and prove that they are still a part of the fallen race of Adam. Even though these people have lived a sin-free life and experienced the goodness of God, they will rebel against Him at the slightest tempting of the Evil One.

This teaching of Jesus concerning the treatment of His brethren reveals a social responsibility that has been placed upon the world concerning its treatment of Jews and Christians. As the end-time approaches, these two segments of the population will receive harsh persecution and mistreatment from the European coalition, led by the Antichrist and his false prophet. In the East, the Islamic Jihad will manifest itself with an unrestrained vengeance.

The rise of Muslim terrorists around the world demonstrates the inextinguishable hatred that exists among them for Jews and American's (Christians). The Islamic mindset considers both as representations of Satan. Even though Muslims will talk about Jesus as a prophet, they consider Christians as the enemy of Islam.

Western nations, seeking to appease the Muslim influence within their borders, have already passed laws that cut at the heart of the Christian belief system, penalizing Believers if they live according to their convictions. In Western European nations, as well as here in America, the Christian God has been removed from any public expression. To say that there exists no anti-God/anti-Christ movement in the world today would be irrational. America and Israel remain the last two Jehovah God fearing nations in the world. Secularism has replaced the Divine influence upon the nations of Europe. Only America and Israel were founded upon a belief and reliance upon the Lord God of Creation.

It is simple to see why America is Israel's last ally. Feeling the pressure of the Muslim influence within its own border, the British Government, which established the Jewish nation in the first place, is pulling away from their dedication to preserve the nation of Israel. How much longer will America support its long time ally? Will this commitment of our nation be unwavering? Will the United States of America produce the backbone that will be needed to stand up for Israel? Probably it will not.

When the government comes against Christians and all who will not support the secular agenda, what are Believers to do? Are we to fight back and demand our rights, or are we to knuckle under and let the world beat us into the ground? Should we run to the caves and hide until this is all over? What are we as Believers to do?

The Lord has not left us without warning or instruction. Christians have a clear mandate from the Lord as what to do when we see this day approaching. The ultimate message from scripture remains simply, "Be Prepared," which means more than placing your faith in Jesus. It means being prepared for the Lord's return. Being "Born Again" prepares you for judgment but not for the "Days of Sorrow." Why did Jesus warn His disciples, who had placed their faith in Him and who were living for him, to be prepared for the last days? Why did He warn them not to be caught unaware (Luke 21:34)? If the Believers are not to go through the trials connected with the "Days of Sorrow," why should they give it a second thought? Well, maybe it is time that they do.

The Gospel, according to Luke, chapter 16:9-29, contains a very complex and somewhat disturbing parable. It is called the parable of the "unjust steward" and, for the most part, it has been overlooked by post-modern Christianity. The very assumption that the Lord would commend an unjust steward demoralizes the Christian mindset and causes many to ignore this important scripture concerning survival during the days of sorrow.

The general thrust of the parable focuses upon judgment and the way the steward prepared to live after it. However, much of the lesson slips past the casual reader because of to the unethical manner in which the steward prepares for life after judgment. In addition to this, the instruction Jesus gives about making friends with unrighteous Mammon surprises the unaware Believer. How could there ever be justification for a Christian making friends with the wealth (Mammon) of unrighteousness? Such a supposition mystifies the conscience and shuts down any other consideration of interpretation or meaning.

In meditating upon this directive of Christ one must remember to keep within the parameters of an end time point of view. The steward knew that he was about to face the scrutiny of his master and that his failures would be discovered. He knew that things were about to get tough and, if he were to survive, he needed a plan. That plan is the focus of the parable.

The unjust steward began to make friends with those who owed a debt to the master. He began by forgiving a portion of the debt, thereby making the debtor obligated to extend a hand of grace unto the steward when he himself would be in debt. At first it seems as if the unjust steward were stealing money from his master, which would seem to be very unlawful and ungodly. How could Jesus ever recommend such behavior? He would never do such a thing. Surely, there has to be more to this story than meets the eye.

Notice that when the unjust steward started making his deals, he did not adjust all accounts the same. One was reduced by fifty percent but the other by twenty percent. When the master discovered what had been done he praised his unjust steward. Why would the master do that? Hadn't the unjust steward just stolen more money from him? Surely, that is not what was happening.

Obviously, the steward must have charged an inflated interest rate to his lord's debtors and pocketed the overcharge into his own purse. Undoubtedly, this was the reason he had to give an accounting in the first place. The amount that he was forgiving was the amount that he had been overcharging his master's clients. Removing his tacked-on surcharges made the debtor owe less, but it did not reduce the remittance that was to go to the master.

The unjust steward could have demanded full payment from the debtors and still raked-off his cut from the top as he had done in the past. However, he concluded that it was better for him to benefit those who were in debt to his master, rather than to try to live off what he could collect in unworthy gain from them. Thus, by making friends with those who were in debt to his master, by forgiving them his inflated part of the indebtedness, he assured that he would be able to have their friendship and assistance in his time of need.

Jesus goes on to say that "the children of this world are in their generation wiser than the children of light." However, Paul said that we "are wise in Christ." How can the children of Light who are wise in Christ not be as wise as the children of this world?

First, it appears that most Christian have their heads so far up in the clouds that they can not see what is happening around them. Having wisdom doesn't mean that one acts in a wise manner. Undoubtedly, Jesus spoke of outward acts and not inward capabilities which Paul addresses. Second, Jesus is not referring to an attitude toward money, but the handling of it. He does not say, "Love unrighteous Mammon." He only says, "Make to yourselves friends of the Mammon of unrighteousness." The Word of God makes it clear that the love of money is the root of all evil but money is a necessity. Some Christians have been fooled into thinking that money is all that is needed to get by in life. As long as one has a nest egg, everything will be all right. In fact, if one has enough money, it is unnecessary to bother the Lord for anything.

The unjust steward realized that, no matter how much money he collected off the top of the accounts he was handling, it would not be enough to sustain his life style. He suddenly realized that if he invested his unjust gains into others, then they would in turn provide an endless resource in his time of need. He was enacting the golden rule, "Do unto others as you would have them do unto you."

In His Sermon on the Mount, Jesus said, "Give and it shall be given unto you." This parable of the unjust steward reinforces this axiom. The unjust steward foresaw greater prosperity and help in the days ahead by benefiting others with the money he had control over. He could not give what was not his to give, but that which he had control over, he released in faith.

Jesus follows this parable with the teaching that a servant cannot serve two masters. He says, "You cannot serve God and Mammon." That statement simply means that you either trust God to meet your needs or you trust your money to do it. You cannot do both.

As the end of the age approaches, many will be tempted to store up great amounts of money to carry them through the trials ahead. The Word of God says that the gold and silver will turn to dust. Jesus again said that we are to put treasures in heaven where rust or decay can not destroy. Believers should invest what they can into the lives of others, notably non-believers. That way, when the Anti-Christ seeks to inflict great harm upon the church, they will have friends to whom they can turn.

The question before us is not really about the judgment of the nations but about us, the Church that is living now. The choice is ours. Being called was God's doing. Being chosen is God's decision, but being faithful is our choice. Are you a faithful and profitable servant of God?

Being saved is about grace "through faith, not of works less any man boast…," but faithfulness is about works, our works. Faithfulness is about what we do with what God has given us. James 2:27 teaches that faith without works is dead. Works identifies where one's faith is placed, Mammon or God.

Let me ask you this: Do you share what you have with others? Do you hoard things for yourself? Do you look for ways to share what you have? Do you seek out those who are in need of that which you have?

I don't have a lot of money. Personally, I don't need a lot. I once told my wife that we could live on less. "Yes, less food!" she replied.

Why has God blessed me with so much? So, I can share it. That is why my house is an open house. We feed many at our table. We share our resources. We have no big savings account upon which to fall back upon. We have enough to take care of small emergencies. We are called to give not collect.

Have we forgotten the instructions of Jesus teach us that it is more blessed to give than to receive? Over and over again the Lord instructs us to be more compassionate and less selfish as we see the Day of Judgment approaching. If the Lord compliments an unjust steward for his compassion for others as his day of judgment approached, how much more so does he require it of faithful stewards?

Everyone needs to prepare spiritually for eternity; even those who have been saved need to prepare. The question is often asked, "Do you know where you will spend eternity?" Maybe the question should be, "How will you spend it? "

The only way to escape the eternal damnation of Hell is through the grace and blood of Jesus Christ. Such Salvation is received by faith. On the other hand, the experiences and privileges one will enjoy in heaven lie in direct correlation with one's works of faith. Minimum Christianity offers minimum reward. Remember, living only by minimum faith could leave you out in maximum darkness.

Truly there is a day known as the "Day of Sorrow." It approaches with an accelerating pace. Are you prepared physically, spiritually, and socially? One day the faithful Believers will reign with Christ and usher in the Millennium. They will be the Called, the Chosen and the Faithful. Will you be part of this glorious group? Jesus said the path that leads to this end is straight and narrow and few there are who find it. Are you looking for it? Time is running out for the human race. It is time to get ready. These are the days of preparation. Now is the time to make plans for the days ahead.

Chapter 9

Personal Defense
Posture
(PDP)

❧

Many readers might consider it oxymoronic to discuss self-defense and faith at the same time. The general view of Christian ideology seems to assume that the Followers of Christ consist of a group of non-combatant, passive, and, somewhat sheepish individuals who must "turn the other cheek" when confronted with any type of evil aggression. To suggest that Believers need to be prepared to defend themselves will, undoubtedly, be rejected by some as outright heresy. Nevertheless, embedded within the teachings of Jesus can be found unquestionable directives for His followers concerning their responsibility for protecting and providing for their family's safety and the security of their possessions (Luke

11:21, 1 Timothy 5:8). Modern Christian pacifism, in all its pleasing meekness and piety, reflects more of a doctrinal creed than a careful contextual interpretation of scripture. Many Christians embrace pacifism because they have been taught by well-meaning teachers that Jesus instructed His followers to be conciliatory and appeasing. Therefore, anyone who takes steps to defend his home and family is viewed as being a demonized, illiterate, radical nut-case who needs to be put on some government watch list.

How did the teachings of Jesus become so distorted? Why are so many Christians buying into this attitude? The teachings of Jesus concerning self-defense are not cloaked in secrecy. In fact, most post-modern Christians do not know what Jesus actually taught concerning this issue. At best, the majority of these Believers occasionally skim over the words of Jesus in their favorite paraphrased version of Scripture. Even those who regularly attend worship services and carry the Authorized Version spend little time in searching the Word of God.

David, the man after God's own heart, understood that one must spend time reflecting upon the Word of God. In Psalms 119:78 he said that he meditated upon the precepts of God. Though not often used in colloquial, everyday language, the word precept means a standard or guide for approved action. It is not the same as the word "law," which implies a precise or direct principle requiring compliance. Precepts require meditation for understanding and acceptance, whereas laws demand obedience. A wise man will meditate also upon the law, but whether he understands it or not, he is held in judgment by it. In other words, ignorance of the law is no excuse for not observing it.

Precepts reveal wisdom through lessons and illustrative teachings which often result from life experiences. Jesus incorporated precepts in his explicatory teachings concerning the Law of Moses to bring to light its meaning and intent for man. In fact, to revive the true intent of the law, which had been lost in the shroud of the religious doctrine, Jesus utilized two instructional methods. His most popular teaching method consisted of parables which were illustrative short stories, but he also used of precepts.

Although similar in context to a parable, precepts fail to follow a story line. Precepts use familiar truths taken from life experiences to teach a simple but yet profound meaning about the law of God. Confusing as it might be to understand the difference between a parable and a precept, remember a parable has a story line and a precept does not. However, both were used by Jesus to reveal God's law to the common man.

One of the strongest teachings of Jesus concerning self-defense is found in Matthew 12:29. Here He taught that even the strongest of men can be defeated if he is first incapacitated. Jesus said, "Or else can one enter into a strong man's house and spoil his goods, except he first bind the strong man and then he will spoil his house." This precept builds upon a common knowledge that before a strong man can be defeated, he first must be bound.

Solomon knew the wisdom of binding things. Ecclesiastes 4:12c reads, "A threefold cord is not quickly broken." Satan knows that if he is to defeat the Church he first must bind the strong man with a threefold cord. What are the three cords used to incapacitate the Believer?

The first cord is called tolerance. When tolerance wraps its web around the heart of the Believer the evangelical arm of the church is rendered inoperative. Tolerance dampens the zeal to witness. The second cord used is political correctness. Wrapped in this deceptive cord of "feelings," the voices of righteousness and integrity are stifled. Fear of offending someone silences the stern warnings concerning the outcome of sin. The third and possibly the most threatening of the three cords is pacifism. When a Believer becomes bound by these three cords, he will be plundered and destroyed.

The forces of evil grow with each passing day. The Church has suffered for over fifty years from the cords of tolerance and political correctness. The cord of tolerance has slowed the growth of the evangelical church. Cords of political correctness have led to the impurity of its laity and ordained leaders. Now, the third cord, the one which seemingly will bind the Believer into an inflexible position, spins its web of deceit within the minds of unsuspecting Believers. The deception of pacifism has been so craftily woven into post-modern theology that most Believers have already accepted the deception that Jesus was an anti-war, anti-weapon pacifist.

Before you throw down this book and call me a phobic-screwball, take some time to review a little history of the Church and the role that the Followers of Christ have had in the development of modern society. It was not anti-war, anti-gun pansies who won the freedom in Europe and delivered the world from the tyranny of the Nazis. Could one truly say that delivering the inlands of the Pacific from the terror of Japan was a Christian act of mercy? Neither could it be said that the pulpits in America leading up to the Revolution were filled with pacifist preachers. Not so!

The Church of today finds itself wrapped in humanistic logic. It is bound by the cords of tolerance, political correctness and pacifism. These three cords are hard to break all at once but taken one at a time, they are breakable. The Church must take a stand for the right to defend one's self. It is time to cut off the cord of pacifism and defend our families, our homes, and our churches.

Luke 11:21 gives a little more insight into this precept that Jesus introduced in Matthew. Luke's account of this event, mentioned earlier, suggest a different insight to what Jesus was teaching. Luke quotes Jesus as saying, "When a **strong man armed** keepeth his *home* his goods are in peace (*personal interpretation*)." Here Jesus emphasized the imperative for self-defense: "strong man armed."

As you meditate upon this, you must ask yourself some probing questions. Was Jesus against a man defending his home? Did Jesus teach that a Believer was not to be armed in self-defense? Did Jesus condemn the strong man for defending his house? What was the common understanding of the precept? Was it understood that a man should protect his belongings? It does not seem that the answers to these questions would lead anyone to conclude that Jesus was teaching pacifism.

One of the strongest texts concerning self-defense is found in Luke 22:36 and 38. It states, "Then said he unto them, 'but now, he that hath a purse, let him take it, and likewise his scrip: and he that hath no sword, let him sell his garment, and buy one....' And they said, 'Lord, here are two swords.' And He said unto them, 'It is enough'." In these verses Jesus places importance upon self-defense. The three areas that Jesus identifies as self-defense preparedness include: first, sufficient funds (the purse), second, clothes (the bag or scrip) and third, a weapon (a sword).

In verse 38, the disciples responded that they already had two swords with them at the time. Notice that Jesus did not scold them or question them about why they were 'packing heat." It was as if it were normal for the disciples to carry a sword.

The two swords which the disciples had were not the long blades of the English knight. These weapons were small curve-bladed knifes that were common in the Middle East at this time. It was lawful to carry such a weapon for self-defense but a saber, similar to those carried by Roman soldiers, would have been illegal. Jesus told Peter to put his sword in its place after he used it against Malchus. He did not tell him to turn it in to the government or to destroy it. However, Jesus makes it very clear to Peter that he was not to draw the sword in an offensive posture, but only in a defensive manner. "He that draws the sword will die by the sword," is not a statement that teaches pacifism, but rather gives instruction in the area of self preservation.

Let it not be forgotten that Jesus instructed his disciples to purchase a sword. Even if they did not have the funds to buy one, the importance of acquiring one required the forfeiting of some unnecessary possession to obtain it. Jesus wanted his disciples to be ready for the persecution that was coming. The weapon of choice would give his followers protection from wild beasts as they hid in the wilderness. It would allow them to secure food for their families and it would give them some protection against thieves.

Many have taken the teaching of Jesus concerning "turning the other cheek" and completely divorced it from the context in which it was given. There is more to turning the other cheek than the pacifists want you to know. First, Jesus was condemning personal retaliation. The text quoted from Exodus concerning an eye for an eye dealt with the responsibility of the magistrate. The law did not apply to personal vendettas, although that had become the commonly accepted view. Second, a slap on the cheek was viewed as a challenge or an insult resulting in some sort of confrontation.

Jesus' teaching can be viewed as a reverse challenge without confrontation. The custom compelled the aggressor to slap the left cheek of the accused with the back of his open right hand. Turning and offering the right cheek required the aggressor to strike with his left hand, which, according to Middle Eastern tradition, he could not do without bringing shame upon himself. The left hand was considered unclean. To touch anyone with the left hand was strictly forbidden.

Either way, this text fails to be a motif for pacifism. Jesus came to fulfill the law, not to destroy it. The Old Testament taught that you were to defend your family, and that it was acceptable to strike a thief who broke into your house. Paul writes in First Timothy 5:8; "But if anyone does not provide for his own, and especially for those of his household, he has denied the faith and is worse than an infidel." Surely this directive would include providing a safe and secure environment for one's family. Proverbs 25:26 states that, "a righteous man who falters before the wicked is like a murky spring and a polluted well." Abraham, the friend of God, took up the sword against the three kings who captured Lot, his nephew. David, the man after God's own heart, resorted to violent acts to protect the property of his father against wild animals. He also defeated Goliath, the threat to the nation of Israel, with a sling shot. Has God now changed into a pacifist grandfather?

Pacifism comes from the doctrine of men, not from the word of God. Rooted deep in Church dogma, it remains a misguiding influence upon many Believers. Well meaning as it may be, the results of such thinking has brought many post-modern Believers to the very brink of surrendering to the destructive forces that seek to destroy not only the Church but also Western Civilization.

Not owning a gun does not automatically make someone a pacifist. There are a lot of people who have no desire to own a gun or any other deadly weapon, but do not object to others who do. They find other ways to follow the teachings of Jesus. To be prepared does not require the purchasing of a weapon. It is not wrong for a Believer not to own a gun, but those who do, find scripture conformation through the teachings of Christ.

If guns frighten you and you know that you could never use one, no matter what, there are other alternatives, like a crossbow or compound bow. Both can easily be acquired at most sporting supplies stories. Pepper sprays and other aerial dispersed defenses have minimum effect but are better than nothing. Self-defense courses also provide some security. A large dog that is trained to protect its owner is a major deterrent to those who have mischief in mind.

Remember that during an extreme emergency, this defensive weapon might also be the only means by which to harvest food or to protect the family from ravenous animals which see humans as a food source. Each individual needs to make their own decision concerning this important issue but be careful not to be judgmental of others if their choices are different from your own. The important point is not the type of defensive device chosen, but that such an item is available and ready for use to protecting one's family.

A self-defense posture includes proactive defenses as well. One of these devices is a safe room. This is a place, usually located in a basement or in the center of the home that can protect the family from biological attacks or pandemic outbreaks. A bathroom, with no outside windows, is an ideal location. No matter its located, this room must be able to be sealed from the outside air. This can be accomplished by using plastic sheeting and duct tape which should be stored in the room. The room should include a communication apparatus, such as a radio. Gas or surgical mask should available in these safe rooms.

Additional information about Safe Rooms is available from FEMA. Request pamphlet FEMA-320. The American Red Cross brochure entitled, "Taking Shelter from the Storm: Building a Safe Room Inside Your House," (L-233), is very helpful in establishing a safe room in your home. Some local contractors specialize in constructing safe rooms in new homes. Check with your local building association to find these contractors.

A pacifist does not take such steps to protect his family. However, a proactive Believer will prepare for the worst but pray for the best. A pacifist does not prepare!

Chapter 10

Engaging the Church

❧

Being prepared personally for the coming of Christ is not the sole intent of this work. This text is also a warning for the Church to get ready for the rapidly approaching "Days of Sorrow." The Church must not only be prepared for the return of Christ but for the days of crisis that precede His Second Coming. If the Church is prepared for these trying days, only then can it faithfully minister in the name of Jesus to a dying and frightened world. Reaching out to souls who are in need still remains a major ministry of the Christian faith.

The Southern Baptist Men's mobile disaster kitchen, which provides meals for hundreds of people, sets a standard for other faith based groups to follow. The success of this ministry prompted this denomination to expand its outreach by training emergency response teams to work in concert with the mobile kitchens. What better way can there be to share the love of God than by taking care of the physical needs of hurting people.

The local church represents a family of Believers and in some respects, has a responsibility to make emergency preparations for its members as well as the community in which it ministers. Providing a food pantry or shelter for evacuees over whelms many small congregations, however, there are a number of ministries which any congregation can activate. One of the simplest forms of providing assistance would be to offer preparedness training classes. Churches ought to make an effort to offer classes in survival skills and emergency preparedness, especially, in regions where natural disasters occur with regularity. Some denominations already offer assistance to the local churches in this type of training.

Local congregations may choose to elect their own emergency preparedness director to oversee this important ministry. Working with local agencies and national organizations, these directors can coordinate emergency and survival training classes for the church and the community. Through an emergency preparedness ministry the local church can fulfill the commission of Jesus to love one another. Offering survival and preparedness training reveals true compassion for others.

Give a fish to a hungry man and he will be hungry again. Teach a hungry man to fish and he will cease to be hungry. Food pantries and clothing closets are admirable pursuits but they fail to provide a lasting assistance. Through preparedness and survival training, the Church is able to minister in a perpetual way the love and grace of Christ.

No one knows the hour nor the day of the next disaster or how severe the damages from it might be. Consequently, there is no way for a church to know how much aid it will need to accumulate. Stockpiling food and supplies for mass distribution is not the most efficient way for a church to minister unless it has vast financial resources. However, teaching its membership how to develop a PSP and FDP is something every congregation can undertake.

In light of all the emphasis the Bible places on personal preparedness, it would seem that the Church has an obligation to encourage individuals and families to make emergency preparations. Individuals as well as families need a survival plan in case of emergencies. The Bible teaches in 1 Timothy 5:8 that those who do not take care of their household are worse that an infidel. Christians live under a divine directive to provide protection and provisions for their relatives, especially those of the immediate family. Providing a Preparedness Plan for emergencies would be a minimum response to this directive.

Gathering supplies and equipment to sustain a family during an emergency presents a challenging task but also knowing how to use them efficiently is just as vital. By offering survival and emergency training, the local church becomes an important support to its membership. By providing classes and workshops on preparedness, the local church will minister in a profound way the compassion of Christ.

Many congregations fail to provide preparedness training simply because they are overwhelmed by the vastness of the subject matter. However, even the smallest congregation can be equipped to assist its members through the help of government and private agencies that are ready to aid the local church in this task.

The American Red Cross provides many opportunities for anyone to become proficient in preparedness. It offers classes in first aid that are unsurpassed by any other organization. It also offers a nationally recognized certified CPR program and other preparedness classes at a minimum cost. Contact the local chapter or the national office about classes which are being offered.

Most counties have an Emergency Management Director. By contacting your local county officials, the church will be able to discover what training or emergency assistance is offered by the government in your area. Many counties have voluntary community emergency teams (C.E.R.T.) that offer a wealth of training. This program is underwritten by FEMA. If your local county is not participating in this program, check with a neighboring county to see if they will assist in training classes. Many C.E.R.T. organizations provide public awareness classes for business and faith-based groups at no cost.

FEMA offers a host of online training courses that can assist the local church in training its membership for disasters and emergencies. These are at no cost and are taken at one's own pace. Some courses offer CEUs for those who need continued education credit hours. These courses can be downloaded and used in a group study session. This government web site is found in Appendix II along with many other helpful addresses of groups and agencies that are there to help the church as well as the individual in preparing for the next emergency.

Another way the local church can express the compassion of Christ is by providing emergency assistance for the elderly, disabled, or any other special-needs member. The local church can do this by establishing a list of members who need assistance in case of disaster. By routinely updating and monitoring such a list, the church establishes a compassionate hands-on ministry of personal care. A list of members who use oxygen or require constant electricity to operated medical devices could be established. These members can then be provided with personal instruction concerning what they are to do in case of emergency or who to contact if a need arises. Establishing a list of alternate care givers and/or family members, along with their contact numbers, offers valuable assistance to special-needs members in case conditions prevail which hinder the church from responding to a crisis. The Bible teaches in James 1:22 that true religion is helping widow and orphans in their distress. Providing assurance that no one will be forgotten or left behind, especially those with special needs, offers peace to the anxious heart.

Local government agencies provide assistance for the special-need population. By dialing 211 one can contact this assistance in times of crisis. The reliability of this assistance during a severe emergency, however, has not truly been tested. By establishing a special-needs emergency list and assigning these members to individual church families who are trained and equipped to handle the special-need requirements, the Church releases the government agency to assist those who have no church or family affiliation.

The Church has been entrusted with a redemptive and an enduring message. It must present both. The importance of redemption should never be neglected, but neither should the message of endurance. Christians are called to endure. The Church has a responsibility to teach and train its membership how to do this. The cry of the Church for centuries has been, "Get Saved!" In these last days should it not also cry, "Get prepared?"

_____ **Chapter** 11

Family Emergency Plan
(FEP)

W hen an emergency occurs, most people rely
upon professional relief organizations or the
government to provide assistance and basic needs.
Americans are very blessed with a government that
stands ready to help in times of disasters. With relief
agencies like the Red Cross and Salvation Army
ready to give aid and comfort, many citizens fail to
take any steps to be personally prepared for a disaster.
However, after most disasters, assistance cannot
reach everyone right away. The relief aid can be
delayed by the disaster itself. Debris, downed power
lines, flooded roads, and other obstacles can hinder
aid from getting to where it is needed. Normally, a
three day laps occurs between the emergency and
when the wheels of relief begin to roll. The best
way to assure your family's safety is to be prepared

before disaster strikes. Disaster can strike quickly and without warning. Suddenly, you are forced to evacuate from your home, workplace or school. In some cases emergencies can put you under quarantine in your home or secured in a safe room. What would you do if basic services – water, gas, electricity or telephones – were cut off? What would you do if gasoline could not be purchased? Do you have enough hard currency to purchase needed supplies if ATMs fail to function or credit cards do not work?

Having a plan in case of an emergency is very important and there is no better place to begin that at home. It is important that each family develops and implements a Family Emergency Plan, but where does one begin?

A successful Family Emergency Plan begins with communication. A thorough discussion among the family about potential emergencies helps establish the reason why a FEP is needed. However, it should be remembered that small children tend to be very realistic with their thoughts, and abstract possibilities often become immediate situations to them. By using biblical guidelines for developing a FEP rather that the need of protecting the family from danger or disasters, adults can ease some of the apprehensiveness that might occur with younger family members. By focusing upon the teachings of scripture for the motivation in developing a FEP rather than preparing for the worse, a positive approach can be given to this somewhat frightening task.

Christians have been instructed to be ready. Preparing an FEP is an important step each Believer can take in obeying Christ's call for readiness. An FEP is not about storing up food and supplies but rather a prescribed course of action to be taken in case of an emergency. The FEP collects phone numbers of emergency agencies, like the police, and emergency medical units that support the local area, neighbors and friends, relatives, and any other family connected relationship.

In Appendix I, there is an FEP card, which is designed to be carried by each family member. It can be photocopied for personal use. This card is designed to contain vital information that family members will need in an emergency.

An important inclusion on this card is a contact person. This person should be someone with whom all members of the family are familiar. Often parents only list themselves as a contact person with the school but sometimes, local crises effects the parents as well. This is why it is important to list an additional contact person out of the local area.

The neighborhood/local meeting place where the family can convene after a crisis or emergency is important. Often in a crisis the family is separated and communications are limited. A prearranged location where to meet will aid in the uniting of the family. This prearranged location should be one the family is familiar with and is easily accessible by all members.

In a local emergency, the contact person who has been assigned to the FEP may be experiencing the same crisis and not be able to respond. This is why it is important to include information concerning an out-of-town contact person. This out-of-town contact most likely would still be able to give assistance, comfort and serve as a communication center for the family in times of a local emergency.

Families with school-age children need to be familiar with the emergency plan of the school. In turn, the school needs to be given the name of the family's contact person in the event that you become incapacitated by the disaster or you cannot be located. You need to know where the school would take the children if they had to leave the campus. Does the campus have a safe room or other disaster preparedness? These things need to be discussed and the resulting information included on the FEP.

A master FEP information sheet has also been included in Appendix I. This worksheet broadens the scope of the information which needs to be included. Information such as evacuation routes along with an alternative location and route is just one example. This sheet also has a place for important information about each member of the family. This should be filled out and a copy kept with the PSP. This sheet also includes plans for family pets. Their safety requires planning, too.

When a crisis occurs, there is seldom enough time to collect the information that will be needed by medical or governmental personnel. If a sudden storm hits in the middle of the night and you have to rush to get out of its path, there will be no time to dig through important papers to gather this information. Having this data in an FEP assures it will be accessible when the need presents itself.

An operational FEP requires that each member understands the importance of the plan. The family should often talk about the FEP and how it is to be implemented. By giving each family member a specific responsibility in implementing the FEP assures that a sense of ownership of the plan will be felt by everyone. At least twice a year the family should participate in an FEP drill to verify all information is up to date and accurate. This would include driving the planned evacuation route.

When an evacuation order is given, an FEP provides vital assistance. With a well developed plan, evacuations become less stressful. By having an alternate route selected in advance allows for trustworthy decisions when major roads become clogged. Having a planned destination is very crucial also. It is hard to head in the right direction if the destination is unknown. By having a preplanned destination and predestinated route, with an alternate, allows family members who are separated during the evacuation to unite more rapidly.

Not knowing when a disaster or emergency will occur, or where each family member will be when the event happens, gives prudence to having an FEP. Not knowing what to do in these times of a crisis causes great anxiety and adds to posttraumatic problems. Having a family plan in place before a crisis occurs aids in the overall family's well-being. Preparing a Family Emergency Plan requires very little work yet offers great benefits. There is no right or wrong way to make a FEP but not having one can cause great stress and undue anxiety.

Having an emergency pack ready which contains a copy of the FEP, one set of clothes for each family member, a first aid kit, bottled water and energy food- such as peanuts, granola bars, or peanut butter and crackers - and some type of communication devise will aid in any emergency. This emergency pack can be part of the PSP but should be readily accessible in any crisis. Some refer to this as a "Grab-in-Go" pack.

This emergency pack is simple to construct. All that is needed is some type of container, like a back pact or duffle bag which has pockets to keep copies of insurance papers, shot records, and other papers like proof of residency. It needs to be compartmen- talized so that medicines, bottled water, snacks, and a set of clothes can be stored and separated. Keep the FEP in an easy accessible place that is accessible to all members of the family.

Jesus gave some enlightenment about the need for an FEP. In Matthew 24:16 He says, "Then let them which be in Judaea flee into the mountains (have a evacuation location): Let him which is on the housetop not come down to take any thing out of his house: neither let him which is in the field return back to take his clothes (an express need for an FEP pack that can be retrieved by any family member). And woe unto them that are with child, and to them that give suck in those days (special need require- ments). But pray ye that your flight be not in the winter (plan for severe weather)...." In Matthew 24: 13 Jesus sanctioned preparedness when he says, "But he that shall endure unto the end, the same shall be saved." Enduring is connected with preparedness, and preparedness is associated with planning.

When will the next hurricane hit the south? When will the next earth quake shake the mid-west? When will the next forest fire destroy a housing development, or when will the next floods rip through the Ohio valley? When will the next terrorist attack strike or the next refinery explode, sending dangerous gases into the atmosphere? No one knows but we all can be prepared.

When will the stock market fall or the dollar fail? When will gas get so expensive that the average wage earner can no longer afford to drive to work? No one knows but everyone can be prepared.

Talking about these things does not offer a very secure feeling but not to be prepared for them causes even more anxiety and stress. Jesus said in Luke 12:32 "Do not be afraid, little flock, for your Father has been pleased to give you the kingdom. Sell your possessions and give to the poor. Provide purses of yourselves that will not wear out, and treasure in heaven that will not be exhausted, where no thief comes near and no moth destroys. For where your treasure is there your heart will be also. Be dressed ready for service and keep your lamps burning, like men waiting for their master to return from a wedding banquet, so that when he comes and knocks they can immediately open the door for him. It will be good for that servant whose master finds them watching when he comes. I tell you the truth, he will dress himself to serve, will have them recline at the table and will come and wait on them. It will be good for those servants whose master finds them ready, even if he comes in the second or third watch of the night (NIV)."

Christians, we have work to do. Get Ready!

APPENDIX I

Reproducible Forms

The following forms may be reproduced for personal use. They are provided as an example and a guide. Each individual person or family has different needs and therefore, not all things have been included. The particular form you use is not the important aspect of personal preparedness. Your list may be simple or as complex as needed. Style does not matter. The important factor remains that precautionary steps are taken.

In Appendix II you will find a list of web sights that can assist you in your personal preparedness. We do not endorse these sights or any of their products. They are provided only as a research source to facilitate your preparedness. Extreme caution should

always be given when researching or buying on the
World Wide Web.

Family Emergency Plan

Make sure your family has a plan in case of an emergency. Fill out these cards and give one to each member of your family to make sure they know who to call and where to meet in case of an emergency. Make as many copies as needed.

Family Emergency Plan

EMERGENCY CONTACT NAME: _____

TELEPHONE:_____

OUT-OF-TOWN CONTACT NAME: _____

TELEPHONE:_____

NEIGHBORHOOD MEETING PLACE: _____

TELEPHONE:_____

OTHER IMPORTANT INFORMATION: _____

DIAL 911 FOR EMERGENCIES

Proverbs 29:25b Whosoever putteth his turst
in the Lord shall be safe

Fold here ·······

ADDITONAL IMPORTANT PHONE NUMBERS AND INFORMATION

_____
_____
_____
_____
_____
_____
_____
_____

Family Emergency Plan

Make sure your family has a plan in case of an emergency. Before an emergency happens, sit down together and decide how you will get in contact with each other, where you will go and what you will do in an emergency. Keep a copy of this plan in your emergency supply kit or another safe place where you can access it in the event of a disaster.

Out-of-Town Contact Name:_____   Telephone Number:_____
Email:_____

Neighborhood Meeting Place:_____   Telephone Number:_____

Regional Meeting Place:_____   Telephone Number:_____

Evacuation Location:_____   Telephone Number:_____

Fill out the following information for each family member and keep it up to date.

Name:_____   Social Security Number:_____

Date of Birth:_____   Important Medical Information:_____

Name:_____   Social Security Number:_____

Date of Birth:_____   Important Medical Information:_____

Name:_____   Social Security Number:_____

Date of Birth:_____   Important Medical Information:_____

Name:_____   Social Security Number:_____

Date of Birth:_____   Important Medical Information:_____

Name:_____ Social Security Number:_____

Date of Birth:_____ Important Medical Information:_____

Name:_____ Social Security Number:_____

Date of Birth:_____ Important Medical Information:_____

Family Emergency Plan:

Write down where your family spends the most time: work, school and other places you frequent. Schools, daycare providers, workplaces and apartment buildings should all have site-specific emergency plans that you and your family need to know about.

Work Location One

Address:_____

Phone Number: _____

Evacuation Location: _____

Work Location Three

Address:_____

PhoneNumber:_____

Evacuation Location: _____

Work Location Two

Address:_____

Phone Number: _____

Evacuation Location: _____

School Location One

Address:_____

PhoneNumber:_____

Evacuation Location: _____

School Location Two

Address:_____

Phone Number: _____

Evacuation Location: _____

Church Location

Address:_____

PhoneNumber:_____

Evacuation Location: _____

School Location Three

Address:_____

Phone Number: _____

Evacuation Location: _____

Other place you frequent

Address:_____

PhoneNumber:_____

Evacuation Location: _____

Important Information	Name	Telephone	Policy Number
Doctor(s):			
Others:			
Pharmacist:			
Medical Insurance:			
Insurance:			
Veterinarian:			

Dial 911 for Emergencies
Dial 211 for Special Need Assistance

PSP CHECKLIST
THE BIBLICAL SUVIVAL GUIDE

Energy/Light Source	Home	Auto	Church
Propane Lanterns			
Flashlights			
Glow stick/flares			
D - Cell			
AA			
AAA			
Generator			
Solar Panels/battery system			
Wind Generator			
FUEL SOURCE:			
Gasoline			
Propane			
Diesel			
COMMUNICATION SOURCES:			
2-Way Radios			
Spray Paint			
Writing Instruments			
Poster Paper			
Duct Tape			
Spiral Notebook			
CRAFT ITEMS:			
Needlework Activities			
Coloring Book/Crayons			
General Art Supplies			

Medical Supplies	HOME	AUTO	CHURCH
NON-PRESCRIPTION MEDICATION:			
Pain relievers/fever reducer			
Anti-Diarrhea Medication			
Antacids			
Anti-nausea medication			
Laxative			
PRESCRIPTION MEDICATION:			
Required- Storable Prescriptions			
Diabetic Medication/Tester			
Extra Eyeglasses/Contacts			
FIRST AID SUPPLIES			
Adhesive Bandages			
5"x9" Sterile Dressing			
Roll Gauze Bandage			
Triangular Bandages			
3"X3" Sterile Pads			
4"x4' Sterile Pads			
Tweezers			
Petroleum Jelly			
Sunscreen			
CPR Breathing Barrier			
First Aid Manual			
3" Cohesive Bandage			
Non-Latex Medical Gloves			
Tongue Depressor (wood)			
2" Adhesive Medical Tape			
Hydrogen Peroxide			
Antibiotic Ointment			
Rubbing Alcohol			
Cotton Balls			

Surgical Mask			
Calamine Lotion			
Aloe Vera Gel			
Thermometer			
Allergy Medications and Creams			
Sanitation and Hygiene	HOME	AUTO	CHURCH
Lip Balm			
Insect Repellent			
Feminine Supplies			
Toilet Paper			
Plastic Garbage Bags			
Plastic - 5 Gallon Bucket w/lid			
Disinfectant/Chlorine Bleach			
Laundry Detergent			
Tooth Paste			
Denture Care Products			
Wash Cloths and Towels (cloth)			
Towels (paper)			
Wet Wipes			
Bar Soap			
Liquid Hand Soap			
Dish Detergent			
Shampoo			
Combs and Brushes			
Deodorants			
Body Lotions			
Body Power			
Food and Water	HOME	AUTO	CHURCH
Baby Foods			
Peanut Butter			
Jellies			
Dehydrated Foods			

Pop Corn			
Pasta			
Dried Beans			
Seeds for Planting			
Water (1 gallon per person per day			
Ready-to-eat Meals			
Canned or Boxed Juices			
Canned or Boxed Powdered Milk			
Dried Fruits			
Canned Nuts			
Dried Cereal or Granola			
Protein or Fruit Bars			
Crackers			
Hard Candy			
Instant Coffee or Tea			
Special Diet Foods			
Rice			
Flours			
Baking Powder			
Vinegar			
Olive Oil			
Dried Beans			
Spices			
Kitchen Tools/ Equipment	**HOME**	**AUTO**	**CHURCH**
Cooking pots (open fire compatible)			
Mess Kits			
Paper Plates and disposable cups			
Knifes (all purpose kitchen)			
Aluminum Foil			
Washable plates and cups			
Plastic Utensils			
Plastic Wrap			

	HOME	AUTO	CHURCH
Plastic Bags (food storage)			
Wash tubs			
Coffee Pot			
Manual Can Opener			
Electrical tape			
General Tools and Equipment	HOME	AUTO	CHURCH
Fire Extinguisher (ABC type)			
Signal Flare/Strobe Light			
Temporary Shelter (tent)			
Plastic Sheeting			
Bedding			
Clothing			
Wood Working Hand Tools			
Combination Tool			
Animal Traps			
Non-Cooking Knives			
Fishing Equipment			

APPENDIX II

❧

http://www.survivalunlimited.com
http://www.fluarmour.com
http://www.globalincidentmap.com
http://www.redcross.org/services/disaster
http://www.usa.gov/topics/usgresponse
http://ready.gov
http://citizencorps.gov/ready
http://prepared.org/children.htm
http://us-cert.gov
http://kids.getnetwise.org
http://scouting.ord/pub/emergency
http://preparenow.org
http://nvoad.org
http://cdc.gov
http://ama-assn.org
http://gov/disaster
http://www.oism.org

Log on our home web page for update information and conferences and speaking engagements.

http://www.biblicalsurvival.com

Printed in the United States
138190LV00001B/38/P